# MARC/AACR2/
# Authority Control Tagging

## A Blitz Cataloging Workbook

### Second Edition

## Bobby Ferguson

LIBRARIES
UNLIMITED
A Member of the Greenwood Publishing Group

Westport, Connecticut ● London

**Library of Congress Cataloging-in-Publication Data**

Ferguson, Bobby.
    MARC/AACR2/authority control tagging : a blitz cataloging workbook / Bobby
    Ferguson.—2nd ed.
        p. cm.
    Includes index.
    ISBN 1-59158-205-9 (pbk. : alk. paper)
    1. Authority files (Information retrieval). 2. Authority files (Information
retrieval)—Problems, exercises, etc. 3. Anglo-American cataloguing rules. 4.
Anglo-American cataloguing rules—Problems, exercises, etc. 5. MARC formats. 6. MARC
formats—Problems, exercises, etc. 7. Descriptive cataloging—Rules. 8. Descriptive
cataloging—Rules—Problems, exercises, etc. I. Title.
Z693.3.A88F47 2005
025.3′2—dc22            2004063831

British Library Cataloguing in Publication Data is available.

Library of Congress Catalog Card Number: 2004063831
ISBN: 1-59158-205-9

First published in 2005

Libraries Unlimited, 88 Post Road West, Westport, CT 06881
A Member of the Greenwood Publishing Group, Inc.
www.lu.com

Printed in the United States of America

The paper used in this book complies with the
Permanent Paper Standard issued by the National
Information Standards Organization (Z39.48-1984).

10 9 8 7 6 5 4 3 2 1

# CONTENTS

# ACKNOWLEDGMENTS

I would like to express my appreciation and gratitude to Lydia Acosta and John Richard of the East Baton Rouge Parish Library; all the Sharps and Fergusons; Ally Aran; Gary Ferguson for help with the wording and proofing, and for his continuing friendship; and my copyeditor, Sharon DeJohn, for all her help and knowledge. Thank you all.

# BLITZ CATALOGING WORKBOOK SERIES

# Introduction

Cataloging and classification are the most important parts of librarianship. Without a catalog, either manual or electronic, a library is no more than a room full of books and cannot provide services to its patrons in a reliable, timely fashion. Other library activities such as acquisition of new materials, interlibrary lending, and reference cannot be accomplished if patrons and staff cannot find out what a particular library contains.

Knowledge of cataloging is important to all librarians, not just catalogers. As more and more libraries become automated, a knowledge of MARC fields and electronic formats, as well as call numbers and subject headings, is essential and will make all librarians more proficient. Using these workbooks should cause you to absorb a lot of information that will be useful to you in any library situation.

As for catalogers, you will find that you cannot do a superior job as a beginning cataloger. Experience is necessary, preferably under an experienced cataloger. These workbooks are intended to reinforce your knowledge of the fundamentals of cataloging. They will help you to understand the MARC format and functions of the various fields and subfields; to evaluate copy cataloging and classification of various formats of materials; to locate errors and inconsistencies; to learn access points and which are the most important; to assign subject headings using both *Library of Congress Subject Headings* and *Sears List of Subject Headings*; to assign call numbers in both Dewey and LC classification schedules; and to evaluate and construct cross-references and authority headings.

# DESCRIPTIVE CATALOGING

## Introduction

Cataloging in an online environment has two basic sets of rules: *Anglo-American Cataloguing Rules*, 2nd edition, 1988 revision, called *AACR2R*, and the Machine Readable Cataloging format, or MARC. *AACR2R* is, of course, the more important of the two, and takes precedence over the MARC format where there are inconsistencies.

MARC was designed to make cataloging usable by computers. Some difficulties are caused by the programming of individual integrated library systems such as NOTIS, Galaxy, Innovation Access, Dynix, and CLSI. For example, *AACR2R* gives rules for notes that require 5xx fields to be entered in a particular order, but not the MARC format's numerical order. Some systems automatically line the fields up in numerical order, thus forcing the MARC cataloging record to take precedence over *AACR2R*. When this happens, the cataloger's hands are tied—there is no way the proper order can be applied. In this workbook the integrated library system will be designed correctly, and *AACR2R* will always take precedence over the MARC format.

This workbook is designed to help you learn the correct way of applying cataloging tools, identifying errors in both original and copy cataloging, and maintaining proper authority control for more complete access.

# 1.

# MARC FORMAT

## Introduction

A knowledge of tags, indicators, fields, and subfields is essential for all catalogers and, indeed, all librarians. The numeric tags tell in computer-recognizable language what information is contained in the ensuing field. Reference librarians will find this helpful in decoding the record. For catalogers, this knowledge is the most important part of automated cataloging. Although *Anglo-American Cataloguing Rules* is the primary tool of original catalogers, knowledge of the computer format is essential for accurate inputting and retrieval of information from bibliographic records.

Indicators are digits found immediately following the three-digit field that "indicate" something to the computer. The chart beginning on page 18 gives the indicators for most fields, and will be useful in the tagging exercises.

Subfields are identified by letters or digits; *a, b,* and *c* are the most commonly used delimiters, and their meaning is field-specific. For instance, in the 245 field (title), *a* indicates the main title, *b* the subtitle, and *c* the statement of responsibility. In the 260 field (imprint), *a* indicates the place of publication, *b* the publisher or distributor, and *c* the date of publication. You will need to use the *MARC21 Bibliographic Format* to help you with the tagging exercises.

Authority control has its own MARC format. The tags and subfields are different from the bibliographic MARC record, and the relationship between the tags is different. Because of this, a separate section on authority control is included in this volume.

## 1.1. Families of Tags

Different tags that begin with the same digit form a group, or family, of tags and are referred to by the first digit followed by "xx". These families are briefly explained below, followed by exercises.

0xx    Primarily coded data to help the computer better utilize information. Usually only a cataloger will understand and/or use these data.

1xx    Main entry fields. This may be a personal name; a corporate name; a conference, meeting, or event name; or a uniform title.

24x    Title fields. This may include a uniform title, a main title, or added titles.

1

25x      Edition and scale fields.

260      Imprint. This is not a family as there is only one 26x field in a record.

3xx      Physical description. Also includes frequency, publication dates, and/or volume designations for serials.

4xx      Series. These may be title or author/title entries, traced or untraced.

5xx      Notes. There are many types of notes. They include bibliographies, contents, summaries, cast or credits, dissertations, and many more, including general notes, which may be anything the cataloger wants to add.

6xx      Subjects. These are personal or corporate names, conferences or events, topics, geographic names, or uniform titles.

7xx      Added entries. These may include, among others, joint authors, illustrators, or editors; corporate bodies; analytical entries; or linking entries.

8xx      Added series entries and other linking entries.

9xx      Local fields. These give library-specific information and may be defined as libraries wish. They may include accession numbers, copy numbers, branch locations, donor information for gifts, date of cataloging, bindery information, or anything else a library wishes to include in the records.

Some data elements dealing with types of names can be found in more than one field. These are assigned two-digit codes, which are added to the first digit of the field in which they appear. Each of these families of tags is designated by an "x" followed by the two-digit code.

x00      Personal names. These may be found as main entries (100), series entries (400/800), subjects (600), or added entries (700).

x10      Corporate names. These may be found as 110, 610, 710, or 810.

x11      Conference or meeting names. These may be found as 111, 611, 711, or 811.

x30      Uniform titles. These may be 130, 630, 730, or 830. They may also be 240, where there is a 1xx main entry present.

## Families of Tags Exercise

Write the tag family on the blank before each of the following types of bibliographic data.

1.1.1.   _____  Subjects

1.1.2.   _____  Imprint

1.1.3.    _____ Series

1.1.4.    _____ Local fields

1.1.5.    _____ Main entry

1.1.6.    _____ Computer utilization fields

1.1.7.    _____ Added series

1.1.8.    _____ Physical description

1.1.9.    _____ Added entries

1.1.10.    _____ Title fields

1.1.11.    _____ Edition and scale fields

1.1.12.    _____ Notes fields

Write the names of the tag families on the line following the tag.

1.1.13.    9xx _____

1.1.14.    0xx _____

1.1.15.    7xx _____

1.1.16.    24x _____

1.1.17.    5xx _____

1.1.18.    1xx _____

1.1.19.    8xx _____

1.1.20.    25x _____

1.1.21.    3xx _____

1.1.22.    6xx _____

1.1.23.    4xx _____

1.1.24.    260 _____

Write the names of the data elements on the blank following each tag.

1.1.25.    x30 _____

1.1.26.    x00 _____

1.1.27.    x11 _____

1.1.28.    x10 _____

Write the tags on the line preceding the names of the data elements.

1.1.29.    _____    Uniform titles

1.1.30.    _____    Corporate names

1.1.31.    _____    Conference or meeting names

1.1.32.    _____    Personal names

# 1.2.    008 (Header) Information, Bibliographic Records

The header in bibliographic and authority records is used to record the basic information such as the date the record was created; whether or not the work is juvenile, fiction, or biographical; or whether it is a government document. This information is given in field 008 and consists of forty character positions numbered 00–39, which contain defined data elements and provide coded information about the record as a whole or about special format aspects of the item being cataloged. Some indexing information is taken from the 008 field rather than the textual fields in the body of the record. Character positions 00–17 and 35–39 are the same for all formats; positions 18–34 are different for each format, with some exceptions. A data element common to more than one format always occupies the same character position in the record. For example, whenever a format has an element defined as **Government publication**, the element is in position 28. The Music format, for example, has no **Government publication** element, so position 28 is used for something else. The Maps format, on the other hand, does have a **Government publication** element, which is in position 28. Positions 26–27 and 29–30 are currently undefined in the Maps format.

Undefined character positions contain either a blank ( ) or a fill character ( | ). Each defined character position must contain either a defined code or a fill character. The characters defined across all formats (positions 00–17 and 35–39), as well as positions 18–34 for books, are given here. All codes (Country of publication code, Language code, and others) are taken from USMARC code lists.

The following lists identify the 40 character positions for the 008 field. The first list identifies character positions used for all materials, regardless of type; the second list identifies the character positions used when cataloging books.

# 008—All Materials

00–05    Date entered on file; indicates the date the record was created; recorded in the pattern *yymmdd* (year/year/month/month/day/day).

06       Type of date/publication status. One-character code that categorizes the type of dates given in 008/07–10 (Date 1) and 008/11–14 (Date 2). For serials, 008/06 also indicates the publication status.

   b—No dates given; B.C. date involved. Each character in fields 008/07–10 and 008/11–14 contains a blank (   ).

   c—Serial item currently published. 008/07–10 contains the beginning date of publication; 008/11–14 contains 9999.

   d—Dead status. 008/07–10 contains beginning date of publication, 008/11–14 contains ending date.

   e—Detailed date; 008/07–10 contains year and 008/11–14 contains month and day, recorded as *mmdd*.

   i—Inclusive dates of collection.

   k—Range of years of bulk of collection.

   m—Multiple dates; 008/07–10 usually contains the beginning date and 008/11–14 contains the ending date.

   n—Dates unknown; each position in 008/07–10 and 008/11–14 contain blanks (   )

   p—Date of distribution/release/issue and production/recording session when different.

   q—Questionable date; 008/07–10 contains the earliest possible date; 008/11–14 contains the latest possible date.

   r—Reprint/reissue date and original date; 008/07–10 contains the date of reproduction or reissue (i.e., the most current date) and 008/11–14 contains the date of the original, if known.

   s—Single known/probable date. 008/07–10 contains the date; 008/11–14 contains blanks (    )

   t—Publication date and copyright date. 008/07–10 contains date of publication, 08/11–14 contains copyright date

   u—Serial status unknown. 008/07–10 contains the beginning date of publication; 008/11–14 contains 9999.

07–10 (Date 1)

   A date specified by the code in 008/06. See the codes in 008/06 for examples and input conventions related to coded date information. As this date is often used for retrieval and duplicate detection, the use of fill characters is discouraged.

11–14 (Date 2)

   A date specified by the code in 008/06. See the codes in 008/06 for examples and input conventions related to coded date information.

15–17    Place of publication, production, or execution. A two- or three-character code that indicates the place of publication, production, or execution. Two-character codes are left-justified and the unused position contains a blank ( ). [Codes for the United States consist of the two-letter ZIP code abbreviation plus *u* for United States. New York, for example, would be coded *nyu*.] Unless otherwise specified, codes are always lowercase letters. See current MARC Code List for Countries.

35–37    Language. A three-character code indicating the language of the item. See current *MARC Code List for Languages*.

38       Modified record. A one-character code that indicates whether any data in a bibliographic record are a modification of information that appeared on the item being cataloged or that was intended to be included in the USMARC record. Codes are assigned a priority, and, when more than one code applies to the item, are recorded in the order of the following list.

       (blank)—Not modified.

    d—Dashed-on information omitted.

    s—Shortened.

    x—Missing characters.

    o—Completely romanized/printed cards in Roman script only.

    r—Completely romanized/printed cards in nonroman script

39       Cataloging source. A one-character code that indicates the creator of the original cataloging record. If the cataloging source is known, it is identified in subfield ≠a of field 040.

       (blank)—Library of Congress

    c—Cooperative cataloging program

    d—Other sources [*most libraries fall here*]

    u—Unknown

## 008—Books

18–21    Illustrations. Up to four one-character codes recorded in alphabetical order that indicate the presence of types of illustrations in the item. Codes are left-justified and each unused position contains a blank ( ).

       (blank)—no illustrations

    a—Illustrations

    b—Maps

    c—Portraits

    d—Charts

    e—Plans

    f—Plates

    g—Music

    h—Facsimiles

i—Coats of arms

j—Genealogical tables

k—Forms

l—Samples

m—Phonodisc, phonowire, etc.

o—Photographs

p—Illuminations

22      Target audience.

(blank)—Unknown or not specified

a—Preschool

b—Primary

c—Elementary and junior high school

d—Secondary (senior high school)

e—Adult

f—Specialized

g—General

j—Juvenile

23      Form of item. One character code specifies the form of material for the item in hand.

(blank)—None of the following

a—Microfilm

b—Microfiche

c—Microopaque

d—Large print

f—Braille

r—Regular print reproduction; Eye-readable print

s—Electronic

24–27   Nature of contents. Up to four one-character codes recorded in alphabetical order that indicate whether a significant part of the item is, or contains, certain types of material. Codes are left-justified and the unused positions contain blanks ( ).

(blank)—No specified nature of contents

a—Abstracts or summaries

b—Bibliographies

c—Catalogs

d—Dictionaries. Also glossaries or gazetteers

e—Encyclopedias

f—Handbooks

g—Legal articles

i—Indexes. Item is or contains an index to material *other* than itself j—Patent document

k—Discographies

l—Legislation. Contains full or partial texts of enactments of legislative bodies or texts of rules and regulations issued by executive or administrative agencies

m—Theses

n—Surveys of literature in a subject area

o—Reviews

p—Programmed texts

q—Filmographies

r—Directories

s—Statistics

t—Technical reports

v—Legal cases and case notes

w—Law reports and digests

z—Treaties

28 Government publication. A one-character code indicating whether the item is published or produced by or for a government agency, and if so, the jurisdictional level of the agency.

(blank)—Not a government publication

a—Autonomous or semi-autonomous component

c—Multilocal

f—Federal/national

i—International/intergovernmental

l—Local

m—Multistate

o—Government publication—level undetermined

s—State, provincial, territorial, dependent, etc.

u—Unknown if item is government publication or not

z—Other

29 Conference publication

0—Not a conference publication

1—Conference publication

30 Festschrift

0—Not a festschrift

1—Festschrift

31 Index [contains index to its own contents]

0—No index

1—Index present

32      Undefined. Contains a blank ( ) or fill character ( | )
33      Literary form

      0—Not fiction (not further specified)

      1—Fiction (not further specified)

      c—Comic strips

      d—Dramas

      e—Essays

      f—Novels

      h—Humor, satires, etc.

      i—Letters

      j—Short stories

      m—Mixed forms

      p—Poetry

      s—Speeches

      u—Unknown

34      Biography

      (blank)—No biographical/autobiographical material

      a—Autobiography

      b—Individual biography

      c—Collective biography

      d—Contains biographical information

# 008 Field, Bibliographic Records, Exercise Set 1

1.2.1.      Code the following dates in *yymmdd* format.

      a.  June 29, 1944        _____

      b.  May 1, 1986        _____

      c.  November 11, 1964        _____

      d.  May 27, 1970        _____

      e.  September 23, 1996        _____

      f.  March 8, 1978        _____

1.2.2.    Write the type of date type, date 1, and date 2 on the appropriate lines.

a.        Published in 1991, reprinted in 1997

____   _____   _____

b.        Three volumes published between 1981 and 1987

____   _____   _____

c.        Work published for the first time in 1997

____   _____   _____

d.        Ongoing monographic series beginning in 1963

____   _____   _____

e.        Published sometime in the 1970s

____   _____   _____

f.        Probably published in the first half of the century

____   _____   _____

g.        Produced in 1973, released in 1986

____   _____   _____

h.        No indication of publishing date

____   _____   _____

1.2.3.    Give the code for the place of publication. You will need the *MARC Code List for Countries* to complete this section.

a.    Missouri        _____

b.    New Jersey      _____

c.    Arkansas        _____

d.    Maryland        _____

e.    Massachusetts   _____

f.    Florida         _____

g.    England         _____

h.    France          _____

i.   China          _____

j.   Vietnam        _____

k.   Bosnia         _____

1.2.4.   Code for the following illustrations. Remember, the codes are recorded in alphabetical order.

a.   Plates, genealogical tables, maps

_____

b.   Charts, photographs, music, plans, portraits

_____

c.   Pictures

_____

d.   Coats of arms, genealogical tables, facsimiles, forms

_____

e.   Samples, forms, plans, pictures

_____

f.   Music, phonodiscs, pictures

_____

g.   Maps, plans, charts

_____

h.   Illustrations, plates, portraits, facsimiles, illuminations

_____

i.   Portraits, illuminations, genealogical tables

_____

j.   Music, maps, charts

_____

1.2.5.   Code for the following audience levels.

    a.   Juvenile fiction   _____

    b.   "Ages 5-7"   _____

    c.   Ages 15 and up   _____

    d.   Adult   _____

    e.   For nurses   _____

    f.   Preschool   _____

    g.   High school   _____

    h.   All ages   _____

    i.   "Grades 4-8"   _____

    j.   "Ages 5-9"   _____

1.2.6.   Code for the form of the item or work.

    a.   Microfiche   _____

    b.   Braille   _____

    c.   Microfilm   _____

    d.   Large print   _____

    e.   Microopaque   _____

    f.   Electronics   _____

1.2.7.   Code for the nature of contents.

    a.   Periodical index   _____

    b.   Discography   _____

    c.   Handbooks   _____

    d.   Catalog of catalogs _____

    e.   Statistics   _____

    f.   Encyclopedias   _____

g.   Legislation          _____

h   Legal cases          _____

i.   Patent document   _____

j.   Bibliography          _____

1.2.8.   Code for the type of government publication.

a.   Local                   _____

b.   Federal               _____

c.   State                   _____

d.   International         _____

e.   Not governmental _____

f.   Multilocal            _____

g.   Multistate            _____

1.2.9.   Code for biography.

a.   Autobiography                                 _____

b.   Collected biography                         _____

c.   Collected autobiography                   _____

d.   Individual biography                       _____

e.   Contains biographical information        _____

f.   Contains no biographical information    _____

1.2.10.   Code for the language of the publication. You will need to use the *MARC Code List for Languages.*

a.   French              _____

b.   Vietnamese        _____

c.   English             _____

    d.    Chinese    _____

    e.    Spanish    _____

    f.    German    _____

    g.    Italian    _____

    h.    Arabic    _____

1.2.11.    Code for type of modified record.

    a.    Shortened record    _____

    b.    Dashed-on information    _____

    c.    Missing characters    _____

    d.    Romanized script/cards    _____

    e.    Unmodified record    _____

1.2.12.    Code for cataloging source.

    a.    Your library    _____

    b.    Library of Congress    _____

    c.    NACO    _____

    d.    Southern University    _____

1.2.13.    Define the following positions. Identify each as G for general (i.e., for all materials) or B for books.

    a.    008/06    _____

    b.    008/30    _____

    c.    008/15-17    _____

    d.    008/29    _____

    e.    008/00-05    _____

    f.    008/35-37    _____

g.   008/18-21   _____

h.   008/39   _____

i.   008/24-27   _____

j.   008/07-10   _____

k.   008/32   _____

l.   008/38   _____

m.   008/11-14   _____

n.   008/31   _____

o.   008/28   _____

p.   008/22   _____

q.   008/34   _____

r.   008/23   _____

s.   008/33   _____

## 008 Field, Bibliographic Records, Exercise Set 2

In the following exercises you are given all the information you need to code the 008 field. Be careful of your spacing, and make sure your codes occupy the correction position. Dots are given for help in identifying character positions.

1.2.14   008   . . . . . . . . . . . . . . . . . . . . . . . . . . . . . . . . . . . . . . .

100   1   ≠a Stringer, Chris.

245   10   ≠a African exodus : ≠b the origins of modern humanity.

250   ≠a 1st ed.

260   ≠a New York : ≠b Henry Holt, ≠c c1996.

300   ≠a xx, 282 p. : ≠b ill. ; ≠c 25 cm.

504   ≠a Includes bibliographical references and index.

1.2.15.  008  . . . . . . . . . . . . . . . . . . . . . . . . . . . . . . . . . . . . . . . . . . . . . . . . . . .

        100  1     ≠a Gorman, Jacquelin.

        245  14   ≠a The seeing glass: a memoir.

        260      ≠a New York : ≠b Riverhead Books, ≠c 1997.

        300      ≠a 255 p. ; ≠c 22 cm.

1.2.16.  008  . . . . . . . . . . . . . . . . . . . . . . . . . . . . . . . . . . . . . . . . . . . . . . . . . . .

        100  1     ≠a Stillman, Jackie.

        245  14   ≠a The new Americans : ≠b how immigrants renew our country.

        260      ≠a Starkville, Miss. : ≠b University of Mississippi, ≠c1994.

        300      ≠a x, 369 p. : ≠b ill., maps ; ≠c 25 cm.

        504      ≠a Includes bibliographical references and index.

1.2.17.  008  . . . . . . . . . . . . . . . . . . . . . . . . . . . . . . . . . . . . . . . . . . . . . . . . . . .

        100  1     ≠a Mayer, Sharon.

        245  10   ≠a Declaration of Independence, the American scripture.

        260      ≠a New York : ≠b Frolic Press, ≠c 1995.

        300      ≠a xxi, 300 p. : ≠b maps ; ≠c 25 cm.

        500      ≠a Includes index.

1.2.18.  008  . . . . . . . . . . . . . . . . . . . . . . . . . . . . . . . . . . . . . . . . . . . . . . . . . . .

        100  1     ≠a Rogers, Elaine.

        245  10   ≠a History of America's murders.

        260      ≠a Columbus, Ohio : ≠b Field Press, ≠c 1996.

        300      ≠a ix, 399 p., [8] p. of plates : ≠b ill., ports. ; ≠c 24 cm.

        504      ≠a Includes bibliographical references (p. 355-387).

1.2.19.  008  . . . . . . . . . . . . . . . . . . . . . . . . . . . . . . . . . . . . . . . . . . . . . . . . . . .

        100  1     ≠a Thorne, John B.

        245  12   ≠a L'histoire de la Louisiane.

        250      ≠a 1st ed.

        260      ≠a Paris : ≠b L'editions Francaise, ≠c 1997.

        300      ≠a xx, 390 p. : ≠b ill. (some col.), maps ; ≠c 29 cm.

        504      ≠a Includes bibliographical references and index.

1.2.20.  008  . . . . . . . . . . . . . . . . . . . . . . . . . . . . . . . . . . . . . . . . . . . . . . . . . . .

        100  1     ≠a Springer, Joshua.

        245  10   ≠a Dinosaurs : ≠b everything too aged.

        250      ≠a 6th ed.

        260      ≠a Provo, Utah : ≠b Mormon Press, ≠c 1993.

        300      ≠a 63 p. : ≠b col. ill., col. maps ; ≠c 24 cm.

        500      ≠a Includes index.

1.2.21.   008   . . . . . . . . . . . . . . . . . . . . . . . . . . . . . .

100   1   ≠a Aarons, Lettie.

245   10   ≠a Ballad of true love : ≠b love is blind, etc.

250   ≠a 2nd ed.

260   ≠a Chicago : ≠b Field Museum Press, ≠c 1997.

300   ≠a x, 179 p. ; ≠c 30 cm.

504   ≠a Includes bibliographical references (p. 167-177) and index.

1.2.22.   008   . . . . . . . . . . . . . . . . . . . . . . . . . . . . . .

100   1   ≠a DeKing, Elizabeth.

245   10   ≠a Cry for me, my darlings.

260   ≠a London : ≠b Chidi Press, ≠c 1997.

300   ≠a 385 p., [36] p. of plates : ≠b col. ill. ; ≠c 30 cm.

504   ≠a Includes bibliographical references and index.

1.2.23.   008   . . . . . . . . . . . . . . . . . . . . . . . . . . . . . .

100   1   ≠a Morrison, Sylvia J.

245   10   ≠a Rage for age : ≠b the increasing elder generation.

250   ≠a 1st ed.

260   ≠a Washington, D.C. : ≠b Dept. of Health, Education, and Welfare ; for sale by the U.S. G.P.O., ≠c 1997.

300   ≠a 65 p. ; ≠c 28 cm.

1.2.24.   008   . . . . . . . . . . . . . . . . . . . . . . . . . . . . . .

100   1   ≠a Van Heusen, Phillips.

245   10   ≠a Beer for all! : ≠b and other campaign promises not kept.

260   ≠a Kansas City, MO : ≠b Beer Industry Press, ≠c 1996.

300   ≠a x, 309 p. : ≠b ill. ; ≠c 28 cm.

500   ≠a Includes index.

1.2.25.   008   . . . . . . . . . . . . . . . . . . . . . . . . . . . . . .

100   1   ≠a Wilder, Genevieve.

245   10   ≠a Mothers know best.

260   ≠a Good Living, AK : ≠b Snow Press, ≠c 1997.

300   ≠a 125 p., [48] p. of plates : ≠b col. ill. ; ≠c 28 cm.

# 1.3.   Indicators

| 100 _ | Personal name | 110 _ | Corporate name | 111 _ | Conference |
|---|---|---|---|---|---|
| 0 | Single forename | 1 | Place name + period | 2 | Phrase |
| 1 | Surname | 2 | Phrase | | |

245 _   1st indicator: Title tracing 1=Yes, 0=No [Title main entry is coded 0]

_   2nd indicator: Number of spaces to skip in indexing

250   Indicators are blank

260   Indicators are blank

300   Indicators are blank

440 _   Series title traced, 2nd indicator, no. of spaces skipped

490 _   Series title not traced, or traced differently
1st indicator: 0 = not traced, 1 = traced differently [If coded 1, 8xx must be present]

500   Indicators are blank

504   Indicators are blank

505 _   1st indicator: 0 = entire contents, 1 = partial contents

520   Indicators are blank

6xx   Second indicator 0 = LCSH, 1 = Annotated cards, 8 = Sears

600   Same 1st indicators as 100 field

610   Same 1st indicators as 110 field

611   Same 1st indicators as 111 field

650   No 1st indicator

651   No 1st indicator

7xx

700, 710, 711   1st indicator same as 1xx; 2nd indicator blank

740   1st indicator number of spaces to skip; [coded zero—no initial articles used]
2nd indicator 2 [analytical entry]

8xx   Series traced differently.

# 1.4.   Tagging Exercise

Add the proper tags, indicators, and subfields to the data given below. The blanks indicate where tags, indicators, and subfields should be placed. Precede each subfield code with a delimiter. You will need to use the MARC21 bibliographic formats, *AACR2R, LCSH,* or other tools. The first one in each section has been done for you.

## Main entries

1.4.1   <u>100</u> 1   ≠a   Dow, Elizabeth.

1.4.2.   1_ _   _ _ _   Vargas Llosa, Mario.

1.4.3.   1_ _   _ _ _   Nebraska. ___ Legislature. ___ Senate.

1.4.4.   1_ _   _ _ _   Nebraska Academy of Sciences.

1.4.5.   1_ _   _ _ _   Kisatchie National Forest.

1.4.6.   1_ _   _ _ _   Magnus, Olaus, ___ 1490-1557.

1.4.7.   1_ _   _ _ _   Spate, Gaspar J. ___ (Gaspar Julius), ___ 1881-1956.

1.4.8.   1_ _   _ _ _   Paul, ___ of Byzantium.

1.4.9.   1_ _   _ _ _   Who (Musical group)

1.4.10.   1_ _   _ _ _   Shreveport (La.). ___ Police Jury. ___ Library Committee.

1.4.11.   1_ _   _ _ _   Regional Planning Council for Southwest Louisiana.

1.4.12.   1_ _   _ _ _   Bible. ___ O.T. ___ Exodus.

1.4.13.   1_ _   _ _ _   Pennyfeather, John, ___ Sir, ___ 1770-1820.

1.4.14.   1_ _   _   Monroe Bowling Tournament ___ (1983 : ___ Monroe, La.)

## Title statements

1.4.15.   245   <u>10</u>   ≠a   Guide to writing tree ordinances / ≠c prepared by Buck Abbey.

1.4.16.   245   _ _   _ _ _   "Blood will tell!" / ___ Joseph Bosco.

1.4.17.   245   _ _   _ _ _   Reflections in time / ___ Elizabeth Crane, editor.

1.4.18.  245 _ _ ___   The vampire companion / __ Katherine Ramsland.

1.4.19.  245 _ _ ___   The "Gimme something mister" guide to Mardi Gras / ___ by Arthur Hardy.

1.4.20.  245 _ _ ___   Tell me more; or, The Hollywood gossip book / ___ by Nancy Davis Reagan.

1.4.21.  245 _ _ ___   The stumpin' grounds : ___ a memoir of New Orleans' Ninth Ward / ___ by Russell E. Wyman.

1.4.22.  245 _ _ ___   ... So I told him no : ___ the trail to the Vice-Presidency / ___ by Al Gore.

1.4.23.  245 _ _ ___   Fort Claiborne / ___ prepared by Cecil Atkinson.

1.4.24.  245 _ _ ___   Hobnails and helmets / ___ William H. Burkhart ... [et al.].

1.4.25.  245 _ _ ___   The analysis of the law : ___ penalties for transgressors / ___ Sir Matthew Hale.

## Publication, Distribution, etc.

1.4.26.  260   *≠a* New York : *≠b* Greenwillow Press, *≠c* [1949].

1.4.27.  260   ___ Washington D.C. : ___ U.S. Dept. of Agriculture : [for sale by the U.S. G.P.O.], ___ 1964.

1.4.28.  260   ___ London : ___ Haynes ; ___ Brookstone, Conn. : ___ Auto Museum, ___ c1997.

1.4.29.  260   ___ [Bohemia, La.?] : ___ L.B. Oppenheimer, ___ 1957.

1.4.30.  260   ___ [Albuquerque] : ___ University of New Mexico Press, ___ 1985.

1.4.31.  260   ___ Toronto ; New York : ___ Bantam, ___ c1952.

1.4.32.  260   ___ [S.l. : ___ s.n.], ___ 1935.

1.4.33.  260   ___ Paris : ___ LeBlanc et cie., ___ 1935, c1899.

1.4.34.  260   ___ Bayou Manchac, La. : ___ [s.n., ___ 19—?]

1.4.35.  260   ___ Alexandria, La. : ___ Alexandria Museum of Art, ___ c1977.

## Physical Description

| | | |
|---|---|---|
| 1.4.36 | 300 | ≠*a* 3v. ; ≠*c* 30 cm. + ≠*e* atlas (301 leaves of plates : maps) |
| 1.4.37. | 300 | ___ 64 p. : ___ maps ; ___ 32 cm. |
| 1.4.38. | 300 | ___ 65 leaves, 102 p., [8] p. of plates : ___ ill. ; ___ 16 cm. |
| 1.4.39. | 300 | ___ xlv, 789 p. : ___ ill., ports., maps (1 fold.) ; ___ 13 cm. |
| 1.4.40. | 300 | ___ 251 p. ; ___ 22 cm. |
| 1.4.41. | 300 | ___ 1 videocassette (22 min.) : ___ sd., col. ; ___ ½ in. |
| 1.4.42. | 300 | ___ 1 microscope slide : ___ glass ; ___ 8 x 3 cm. |
| 1.4.43. | 300 | ___ 1 game (15 pieces) : ___ col., cardboard ; ___ 9 x 12 in. |
| 1.4.44. | 300 | ___ v. : ___ ill., maps ; ___ 28 cm. |
| 1.4.45. | 300 | ___ 2 film reels (60 min. ea.) : ___ sd., b&w ; ___ 16 mm. |
| 1.4.46. | 300 | ___ ii, 14, vi, 61 p. : ___ ill., facsims. ; ___ 12 x 16 cm. |
| 1.4.47. | 300 | ___ 1 score : ___ 16 p. of music ; ___ 28 cm. + ___ 1 sound disk. |
| 1.4.48. | 300 | ___ 1 v. (various pagings) ; ___ 26 cm. |
| 1.4.49. | 300 | ___ 1 sound disc (65 min.) : ___ digital, stereo. ; ___ 4 3/4 in. |

## Notes

| | | |
|---|---|---|
| 1.4.50 | 5*00* | ≠*a* Title from disk label. |
| 1.4.51. | 5__ | ___Summary: Biography of Shaquille O'Neal. |
| 1.4.52. | 5__ | ___With: Only in your arms / Lisa Kleypas. |
| 1.4.53. | 5__ | ___Includes discography (p. 547-569). |
| 1.4.54. | 5__ | ___Title supplied by cataloger. |
| 1.4.55. | 5__ | ___Reprint. Originally published: Boston : Grey, 1896. |
| 1.4.56. | 5__ | ___Cast: Ronald Reagan, Bill Clinton, George W. Bush. |

1.4.57.    5__ _       ___Contents: Hey look me over -- Louisiana hayride -- Cajun
two-step -- When the saints go marching in -- Bayou blues --
LSU Alma Mater.

1.4.58.    5__          ___Ph.D. (Library Science)—Duke University, 1978.

1.4.59.    5__          ___Includes index.

1.4.60.    5__          ___Editor, 1987- : Bobby Ferguson.

1.4.61.    5__          ___Introduction -- ___Questioning Kubrick's clockwork / S. Y.
McDougal -- ___ Clockwork ... ticking / ___ R. Kolker -- Cultural
productions / ___ J. Staiger -- ___ Erotics of violence / ___ M.
DeRosia -- ___ Art cinema / ___ K. Gabbard.

## Subject Descriptors

1.4.62    *6<u>00</u> 1*      *≠a* Lincoln, Abraham, *≠d* 1809-1865.

1.4.63.    6__ _ _     ___ Gardening ___ Louisiana ___ New Orleans.

1.4.64.    6__ _ _     ___ Louisiana. ___ Office of the Lieutenant Governor.

1.4.65.    6__ _ _     ___ Cookery (Oysters)

1.4.66.    6__ _ _     ___ Daughters of the Confederacy. ___ Louisiana Chapter.
___ Baton Rouge Post.

1.4.67.    6__ _ _     ___ Port Allen (La.) ___ Politics and government.

1.4.68.    6__ _ _     ___ Alexandria (La.) ___ History ___ Civil War, 1861-1865.

1.4.69.    6__ _ _     ___ Lawrence, Elizabeth, ___ 1904-1985.

1.4.70.    6__ _ _     ___ Physically handicapped artists ___ Louisiana.

1.4.71.    6__ _ _     ___ Burford family.

1.4.72.    6__ _ _     ___ Lafourche Parish (La.) ___ Description and travel.

1.4.73.    6__ _ _     ___ Lafayette Parish (La.). ___ Office of the Mayor.

1.4.74.    6__ _ _     ___ New Tickfaw Baptist Church (Livingston Parish, La.)

1.4.75.    6__ _ _     ___ Joan, ___ of Arc, Saint.

1.4.76.   6__ _ _   ___ Pilottown (La.) ___ History.

1.4.77.   6__ _ _   ___ Hunter, Bruce, ___ 1958-

1.4.78.   6__ _ _   ___ East Feliciana Parish (La.) ___ Economic aspects.

1.4.79.   6__ _ _   ___ Hurricanes ___ Louisiana ___ Cheniere Caminada.

1.4.80.   6__ _ _   ___ Grand Isle Tarpon Rodeo ___ (26th : ___ 1979)

1.4.81.   6__ _ _   ___ Bible. ___ O.T. ___ Genesis.

## Full records

The records below are full bibliographic records. Although there are lines for you to use in identifying fields, indicators, and subfields, there are no examples. Use the preceding exercises to help fill in the full records.

### 1.4.82.

110 _ _   ___ Alabama. ___ Alcoholic Beverage Control Board.

245 _ _   ___ Annual beer report / ___ Alabama Alcoholic Beverage Control Board.

260       ___ Montgomery, Ala. : ___ The Board.

300       ___ v. ; ___ 28 cm.

310       ___ Annual

500       ___ Description based on: October 1, 1977-Sept. 30, 1978.

500       ___ Title from cover.

500       ___ Report year ends Sept. 30.

650 _ _   ___ Brewing industry ___ Alabama ___ Statistics.

### 1.4.83.

245 _ _   ___ Marching bands & corps.

246 _ _   ___ Marching bands and corps

260       ___ [Jacksonville, Fla. : ___ River City Publications], ___ 1967-

300      ___ v. : ___ ill. ; ___ 28 cm.

310      ___ Monthly.

362 _    ___ 1967-

500      ___ Includes index.

650 _ _   ___ Bands (Music)

## 1.4.84.

100 _     ___ Milne, A. A. ___ (Alan Alexander), ___ 1882-1956.

245 _ _   ___ The house at Pooh Corner / ___ by A.A. Milne ; illustrated by Kate Greenaway.

260      ___ Chicago, Ill. : ___ Children's Press, ___ c1983.

300      ___ 128 p. : ___ ill. ; ___ 21 cm.

440 _ _   ___ World's greatest classics

700 _     ___ Greenaway, Kate.

## 1.4.85.

100 _     ___ Grahame, Kenneth.

245 _ _   ___ The wind in the willows / ___ by Kenneth Grahame ; illustrated by Robert J. Lee.

260      ___ New York : ___ Dell, ___ 1973, c1969.

300      ___ 244 p. : ___ ill. ; ___ 19 cm.

500      ___ "A Yearling book."

The next group of bibliographic records has only the first digit of the tag. You are to supply the complete tag, the indicators, and the subfields. Lines are given for your assistance in placing subfield tags.

**1.4.86.**

1_ _      ___ Alford, Gilbert K.

2_ _ _    ___ Alford ancestors and descendants : ___ Jacob and Alvina Alford, the Allfords, and related families / ___ by Gil and Anna Alford.

2__       ___ Rev. ed., with corrections.

2__       ___ [S.l.] : ___ G.K. Alford, ___ [1986?]

3__       ___ x, 279 p. : ___ ports., facsims., geneal. tables ; ___ 28 cm.

5__       ___ Includes indexes.

6_ _ _    ___ Alford family.

6_ _ _    ___ Red River Parish (La.) ___ Genealogy.

6_ _ _    ___ Marriage records ___ Louisiana ___ Red River Parish.

7_ _ _    ___ Alford, Anna.

**1.4.87.**

1_ _      ___ Stratton, Joanna L.

2_ _ _    ___ Pioneer women : ___ voices from the Kansas frontier / ___ Joanna L. Stratton ; introduced by Arthur M. Schlesinger, Jr.

2__       ___ 1st ed.

2__       ___ New York : ___ Simon & Schuster, ___ c1981.

3__       ___ 319 p., [16] leaves of plates : ___ ill. ; ___ 24 cm.

5__       ___ Includes bibliographical references (p. [305]-307) and index.

6_ _ _    ___ Women ___ Kansas ___ History.

6_ _ _    ___ Pioneers ___ Kansas ___ History.

### 1.4.88.

2_ _ _    ___ The Bishop's bounty / ___ compiled by The Bishop's Bounty Cookbook
Committee, Saint Mary's Parents' Group, Inc., Saint Mary's Training School
for Retarded Children.

2__          ___ Alexandria, La. : ___ Saint Mary's Parents' Group, ___ c1987.

3__          ___ 318 p. : ___ ill. ; ___ 24 cm.

5__          ___ Includes index.

6_ _ _    ___ Cookery, American ___ Louisiana style.

7_ _ _    ___ Saint Mary's Training School for Retarded Children (Alexandria, La.).
___ Saint Mary's Parents' Group.

### 1.4.89.

2_ _ _    ___ Les blues de Balfa ___ [videorecording] : ___ with Cajun visits /
Visites Cajun.

2__          ___ San Francisco, Calif. : ___ Aginsky Productions, ___ c1983, c1981.

3__          ___ 1 videocassette (20, 16 min.) : ___ sd., col. ; ___ 1/2 in.

5__          ___ VHS format.

5__          ___ Summary: The story of the Balfa Brothers, and a visit to Cajun country.

6_ _ _    ___ Cajuns ___ Louisiana.

6_ _ _    ___ Balfa, Dewey.

6_ _ _    ___ Balfa Brothers (Musical group)

7_ _ _    ___ Cajun visits.

7_ _ _    ___ Visites Cajun.

The last two bibliographic records have no tags, no indicators, no subfields, and no lines to help
you place the subfield delimiters in the correct places. Use the preceding examples, and you're
on your own. Good luck!

## 1.4.90.

_ _          Darensbourg, Joe, 1906-1985.

_ _ _ _      Jazz odyssey : the autobiography of Joe Darensbourg / as told to Peter Vacher.

_ _ _ _      Telling it like it is

_ _ _        Baton Rouge : Louisiana State University Press, 1988, c1987.

_ _ _        vi, 231 p., [32] p. of plates : ports. ; 25 cm.

_ _ _        Includes bibliographical references (p. [197]-207) and index.

_ _ _        Published in England under the title: Telling it like it is.

_ _ _ _      Darensbourg, Joe, 1906-1985.

_ _ _ _      Jazz musicians Louisiana New Orleans.

_ _ _ _      Vacher, Peter, 1937-

## 1.4.91.

_ _ _        Kilbourne, Richard Holcomb.

_ _ _ _      A history of the Louisiana Civil Code : the formative years, 1803-1839 /
             Richard Holcomb Kilbourne, Jr.

_ _ _        [Baton Rouge] : Publications Institute, Paul M. Hebert Law Center,
             Louisiana State University, c1987.

_ _ _        xv, 268 p. ; 24 cm.

_ _ _        "Prepared under the auspices of the Center of Civil Law Studies."-- t.p.

_ _ _        Includes bibliographical references and index.

_ _ _ _      Civil law Louisiana History.

_ _ _ _      Civil law Louisiana Codification History.

_ _ _ _      Paul M. Hebert Law Center.

# 1.5.  Series

A series is a group of separate bibliographic items that are related to each other in some manner and that may or may not be numbered. A series may be a group of articles, memoirs, essays, or other writings issued in sequence, or a separately numbered sequence of volumes. It may be by a single author or by many authors. The name of a series may indicate the subject matter or the publisher that the items have in common, or it may be a generic designation such as Report, Bulletin, or Proceedings. The authorized form of the series name may be different from the way it is printed on the item being cataloged. Using a series tracing gives searchers another access point in the bibliographic record.

There are five fields for series statements in the MARC format.

400  Added entry, personal name

410  Added entry, corporate name

411  Added entry, meeting name

440  Added entry, title

490  Series statement traced differently or not traced at all

When a 490 series statement is used, the first indicator position tells whether the series is not traced (**0**) or is traced differently (**1**). When a series is traced differently, an 8XX field MUST be present in the record.

Coding for the different types of series statements is given below, followed by exercises to reinforce your knowledge of the codes.

## 400  Series Statement/Added Entry—Personal Name

**Indicators**

**First:** Type of personal name entry element
0—Forename
1—Surname
3—Family surname

**Second:** Pronoun represents main entry. A value that indicates whether a possessive pronoun is used to represent the author of the series
0—Main entry not represented by pronoun
1—Main entry represented by pronoun. The author portion of the series statement contains a possessive pronoun that refers to the name in the 1XX field. The first indicator value is based on the type of name entry element in the 1XX field.

**Subfield Codes**

a—Personal name

b—Numeration

c—Titles and other words associated with a name

d—Dates associated with a name

e—Relator term

f—Date of a work

g—Miscellaneous information

k—Form subheading

l—Language of a work

n—Number of part/section of a work

p—Name of part/section of a work

t—Title of a work

u—Affiliation

v—Volume number/sequential designation

x—International Standard Serial Number

4—Relator code

6—Linkage

**Examples:**

400  10  ≠a Wines, David G., ≠d 1940- . ≠t Ideas for self-employment

400  10  ≠a Shakespeare, William, ≠d 1564-1616. ≠t Poems

400  11  ≠a Her ≠t Travels in many lands, ≠v vol. 16

400  11  ≠a His ≠t Letters from Kathmandu

# 410  Series Statement/Added Entry—Corporate Name

**Indicators**

**First:**  Type of corporate name entry element
0—Inverted name
1—Jurisdiction name
2—Name in direct order [*phrase heading*]

**Second:**  Pronoun represents main entry
0—Main entry not represented by pronoun
1—Main entry represented by pronoun

**Subfield Codes**

a—Corporate name or jurisdiction name as entry element

b—Subordinate unit

c—Location of meeting

d—Date of meeting or treaty signing

e—Relator term

f—Date of a work

g—Miscellaneous information

k—Form subheading

l—Language of a work

n—Number of part/section/meeting

p—Name of part/section/meeting

t—Title of a work

u—Affiliation

v—Volume number/sequential designation

x—International Standard Serial number

4—Relator code

6—Linkage

## Examples

410 10 ≠a Jefferson (Tex.). ≠b Office of the Mayor. ≠t Historic buildings and their contents, ≠v v. 7

410 11 ≠a Its ≠t Research bulletin, ≠v 78-RB-3

410 21 ≠a Its ≠t Report ; ≠v no. 1 ≠x 0141-9676

# 411 Series Statement/Added Entry—Meeting Name

**Indicators**

First: Type of meeting name entry element
0—Inverted name
1—Jurisdiction name
2—Name in direct order [*phrase heading*]

Second: Pronoun represents main entry
0—Main entry not represented by pronoun
1—Main entry represented by pronoun

**Subfield Codes**

a—Meeting name or jurisdiction name as entry element

c—Location of meeting

d—Date of meeting

e—Subordinate unit

f—Date of a work

g—Miscellaneous information

k—Form subheading

l—Language of a work

n—Number of part/section/meeting

p—Name of part/section/meeting

q—Name of meeting following jurisdiction name entry element

t—Title of a work

u—Affiliation

v—Volume number/sequential designation

x—International Standard Serial number

4—Relator code

6—Linkage

### Examples

411  10      ≠a Chicago. ≠q Cartography Conference, ≠d 1974. ≠t Map ≠v no. 10
≠x 0000-0000

411  10      ≠a International Labor Conference. ≠t Bulletin

411  21      ≠a Its ≠t Proceedings, ≠v v. 2

## 440   Series Statement/Added Entry—Title

### Indicators

**First:**      Undefined
(Contains a blank)

**Second:**   Nonfiling characters
0–9—Number of nonfiling characters present. *[Common cataloging practice, as recommended by AACR2R, is to omit initial articles which are disregarded in sorting and filing; thus, values 1-9 are unlikely to be used in field 440.]*

### Subfield Codes

a—Title

n—Number of part/section of a work

p—Name of part/section of a work

v—Volume number/sequential designation

x—International Standard Serial number

6—Linkage

### Examples

440  _0      ≠a Collection africaine

440  _0      ≠a Okonomische Studien ; ≠v Bd. 22

440 _0    ≠a Pediatric clinics of North America ; ≠v v. 2, no. 4

440 _0    ≠a Journal of polymer science. ≠n Part C, ≠p Polymer symposia ; ≠v no. 39

440 _0    ≠a Rare book tapes. ≠n Series 1 ; ≠v 5

440 _0    ≠a Janua linguarum. ≠p Series major, ≠x 0075-3114 ; ≠v 100

440 _0    ≠a Romanica Gothoburgensia, ≠x 0080-3683 ; ≠v 12, 16

# 490   Series Statement/Traced Differently or Not at All

### Indicators

**First:**    Specifies whether series is traced

0—Series not traced

1—Series traced differently. Record contains a corresponding 800-830 series added entry field

**Second:**   Undefined; contains a blank ( )

### Subfield Codes

a—Series statement; a series title that may also contain a statement of responsibility, other title information, dates, or volume numbers preceding or appearing as part of the title

1—Library of Congress call number; an LC series call number that is used for a serial that has been issued as part of the series

v—Volume number/sequential designation

x—International Standard Serial number

6—Linkage

### Examples

490 0_    ≠a Pelican books

490 0_    ≠a Computer indexed marriage records

490 1_    ≠a Uniform crime reports

490 1_    ≠a Department of the Army pamphlet ; ≠v 27-50

490 1_    ≠a [1981-]: Reference works

490 1_    ≠a Bulletin / U.S. Department of Labor, Bureau of Labor Statistics

490 1_    ≠a Annual census of manufactures = ≠a Recensement des manufactures. ≠x 0315-5587

490 1_    ≠a Map / Geological Survey of Alabama ; ≠v 158, plate 3

490 1_    ≠a West Virginia University bulletin ; ≠v ser. 74, no. 11-3. ≠a Bulletin / Experiment Station, West Virginia University ; ≠v 111

# 800   Series Added Entry—Personal Name

### Indicators

| | | |
|---|---|---|
| **First:** | Type of personal name entry element | |
| | 0—Forename | |
| | 1—Surname | |
| | 3—Family surname | |
| **Second:** | Undefined. Contains a blank. | |

### Subfield Codes

a—Personal name
b—Numeration
c—Titles and other words associated with a name
d—Dates associated with a name
e—Relator term
f—Date of a work
g—Miscellaneous information
h—Medium *[general material designator for media]*
k—Form subheading
l—Language of a work
m—Medium of performance for music
n—Number of part/section of a work
o—Arranged statement for music
p—Name of part/section of a work
q—Fuller form of name
r—Key for music
s—Version
t—Title of a work
u—Affiliation
v—Volume number/sequential designation
4—Relator code
6—Linkage

### Examples:

800  1_    ≠a Berenholtz, Jim, ≠d 1957- ≠t Teachings of the feathered serpent ; ≠v bk. 1

800  1_    ≠a Poe, Edgar Allan, ≠d 1809-1849. ≠t Works. ≠l German. ≠f 1922. ≠s Rosl ; ≠v 1. Bd.

800  1_    ≠a Joyce, James, ≠d 1882-1941. ≠t James Joyce archive

800  1_    ≠a Darnell, Jack. ≠t Edible wild plants of the planet earth

800  1_    ≠a Armstrong, Louis, ≠d 1900-1971. ≠4 prf ≠t Louie Armstrong (Universal City Studios) ; ≠v 6

# 810  Series Added Entry—Corporate Name

## Indicators

**First:**  Type of corporate name entry element
0—Inverted name
1—Jurisdiction name
2—Name in direct order *[Phrase heading]*

**Second:**  Undefined. Contains a blank.

## Subfield Codes

a—Corporate name or jurisdiction name as entry element
b—Subordinate unit
c—Location of meeting
d—Date of meeting or treaty signing
e—Relator term
f—Date of a work
g—Miscellaneous information
h—Medium
k—Form subheading
l—Language of a work
m—Medium of performance for music
n—Number of part/section/meeting
o—Arranged statement for music
p—Name of part/section/meeting
r—Key for music
s—Version
t—Title of a work
u—Affiliation
v—Volume number/sequential designation
4—Relator code
6—Linkage

## Examples

810 2_     ≠a John Bartholomew and Son. ≠t Bartholomew world travel series ; ≠v 10

810 2_     ≠a Central Institute of Indian Languages. ≠t CIIL linguistic atlas series ; ≠v 1

810 2_     ≠a European Court of Human Rights. ≠t Publications de la Cour europeenne des droits de l'homme. ≠n Serie A, ≠p Arrets et decisions ; ≠v vol. 48

810 1_     ≠a United States. ≠b Army Map Service. ≠t A.M.S., ≠v Z201

# 811    Series Added Entry—Meeting Name

## Indicators

**First:**    Type of meeting name entry element
0—Inverted name
1—Jurisdiction name
2—Name in direct order [*phrase heading*]

**Second:**    Undefined. Contains a blank.

## Subfield Codes

a—Meeting name or jurisdiction name as entry element
c—Location of meeting
d—Date of meeting
e—Subordinate unit
f—Date of a work
g—Miscellaneous information
h—Medium
k—Form subheading
l—Language of a work
n—Number of part/section/meeting
p—Name of part/section/meeting
q—Name of meeting following jurisdiction name entry element
s—Version
t—Title of a work
u—Affiliation
v—Volume number/sequential designation
4—Relator code
6—Linkage

## Examples

811 2_     ≠a International Congress of Romance Linguistics and Philology
≠n (17th : ≠d 1983 : ≠e Aix-en-Provence, France). ≠t Actes du XVIISme
Congress International de linguistique et philologie romanes ; ≠v vol. no. 5

811 2_     ≠a International Congress of Nutrition ≠n (11th : ≠d 1978 : ≠c Rio de
Janeiro, Brazil). ≠t Nutrition and food science ; ≠v v. 1

811 2_     ≠a Delaware Symposium on Language Studies. ≠t Delaware symposia on
language studies ; ≠v 4

# 830   Series Added Entry—Uniform Title

## Indicators

**First:**   Undefined. Contains a blank.

**Second:**   Nonfiling characters
0–9—Number of nonfiling characters present. *[Common cataloging practice, as recommended by AACR2R, is to omit intiial articles which are disregarded in sorting and filing, thus, values 1-9 are unlikely to be used in field 830.]*

## Subfield Codes

a—Uniform title
d—Date of treaty signing
f—Date of a work
g—Miscellaneous information
h—Medium
k—Form subheading
l—Language of a work
m—Medium of performance for music
n—Number of part/section of a work
o—Arranged statement for music
p—Name of part/section of a work
r—Key for music
s—Version
t—Title of a work *[a title-page title of a work]*
v—Volume number/sequential designation
6—Linkage

## Examples

830 _0     ≠a Resources information series

830 _0     ≠a Imago (Series)

830 _0     ≠a Sport (International Union of Students. Physical Education and Sports Dept.) ; ≠v v. 10

830 _0     ≠a Monograph (University of California, Los Angeles. Dept. of Continuing Education in Health Sciences)

830 _0     ≠a Musica de camera (Oxford University Press) ; ≠v 72

830 _0     ≠a Basic nursing skills (Robert J. Brady Company) ; ≠v tape 14

830 _0     ≠a Teenage years.  ≠h [videorecording]

## Series Exercise

Take the following series entries and reformat them for each tag given. Watch the indicators and construct the entries accordingly.

1.5.1.   440 _0   ≠a Rechtschistorisch Instituut (Series). ≠n Serie 1

490 0_   _____

1.5.2.   810 20   ≠a State University of New York. ≠t SUNY series in new directions in crime and justice studies.

440 _0   _____

1.5.3.   490 1_   ≠a Defense of usury / Jeremy Bentham, 1748-1832.

800 1_   _____

440 _0   _____

1.5.4.   490 1_   ≠a AAR studies in religion (American Academy of Religion)

440 _0   _____

810 2_   _____

1.5.5.   400 10   ≠a Moyes, Patricia. ≠t Inspector Henry Tibbett mystery

440 _0   _____

In the next group of exercises you are given author and/or series title information. Use the information to create the series entry specified by the tag you are given. Use correct subfield delimiters. You will not ordinarily use all tags asked for in a single record. They are just given for practice in formatting series entries.

1.5.6.   Author: Lane, Roger.
Series title: History of crime and criminal justice series

400 10   _____

1.5.7.   Author: Horne, Diane.
Series title: Prehistoric animals, volume 3

440 _0   _____

1.5.8.   Author: Probity, Suellen.
Series title: Medical problems
Sub-series title: Part 2, Blood problems

490 1_   _____

_____

800 1_   _____

_____

1.5.9.   Author: Smith, J. Wesley.
Series title: Contemporary questions

490 0_   _____

1.5.10.   Author: Lambert, Stephen E.
Series title: VGM career books
Publisher: VGM Career Horizons

490 1_   _____

830 1_   _____

1.5.11.   Author: Watters, Thomas R.
Series title: Smithsonian guides

440 _0   _____

1.5.12.   Author: Muddy, Juan Bigge.
Series title: A Macmillan reference book

490 1_   _____

830 _0   _____

1.5.13.   Author: Conover, Ernie.
Series title on cover: Woodworking plans series
Series title on title page: Betterway woodworking plans series

490 0_   _____

490 1_   _____

830 _0   _____

1.5.14.  Author: Wiencek, Henry.
Series title from title page: Volume one of The Smithsonian guide to historic America

440 _0 _____

1.5.15.  Author: Steinberg, Eve P.
Series title: Civil service test tutor, Arco Publishing House

490 1_ _____

830 _0 _____

1.5.16.  Author: Freeman, Kerry A.
Series title: Chilton Book Company, Chilton's total car care

440 _0 _____

490 0_ _____

1.5.17.  Author: Mitchell Manuals, inc.
Series title: Mitchell manuals for the automotive professional

440 _0 _____

1.5.18.  Author: Zapata, Hector.
Series title from cover: Louisiana State University Agricultural Center,
Louisiana Agricultural Experiment Station, Dept. of Agricultural Economics
and Agribusiness, Research Report.
Series title from title page: D.A.E. research report

440 _0 _____

490 0_ _____

1.5.19.  Author: Henning, Steven Alan.
Series title from cover: Department of Agricultural Economics and Agribusiness,
Louisiana State University Agricultural Center, Louisiana Agricultural
Experiment Station, information series
Series title from title page: A.E.A. information series

490 1_ _____

830 _0 _____

1.5.20.   Author: Babin, Eric.
Series title: Guitar tunes for country players

490 1_   _____

800 1_   _____

# 1.6.   Error Identification Exercise

There is one error on each line. The errors will be in the tag, the indicators, or the subfields. Circle the error, then write the correction on the line.

1.6.1.   100 1      ≠a Smith, John, ≠z 1956-                    _____

1.6.2.   110 1      ≠a Garcia Williams, John.                   _____

1.6.3.   110 2      ≠a Port Allen (La.). ≠b Parish Council.     _____

1.6.4.   100 2      ≠a Minnie Pearl, ≠d 1921–1967.             _____

1.6.5.   111 1      ≠a Basketball championship ≠d (1995)        _____

1.6.6.   240 12     ≠a A dictionary of dogs.                    _____

1.6.7.   245 10     ≠a The horse runs / ≠c John Equus.          _____

1.6.8.   245 10     ≠b Everybody wins! / ≠c Polly Tishan.       _____

1.6.9.   246 14     ≠a You @#$%^&*!!!                            _____

1.6.10.  245 12     ≠a A man for all seasons / ≠b Jim Doe.      _____

1.6.11.  260        ≠a New York : ≠b c1996.                     _____

1.6.12.  260        ≠a Libraries Unlimited, ≠c c1996.           _____

1.6.13.  260        ≠a Converse, La. : ≠b Lewis Pub., ≠d c1990. _____

1.6.14.  260 0      ≠a Gem, KS : ≠b J.W. Pub. Co., ≠c c1982.    _____

1.6.15.  300        ≠a 123 p. : ≠c ill. ; ≠c 22 cm.             _____

1.6.16.  300        ≠a 54 p. ; ≠b 25 cm.                        _____

1.6.17.  300        ≠b 2 v. ; ≠c 26 cm.                         _____

1.6.18.  300        ≠a 145 p. : ≠b maps, ill. ; ≠c1965-         _____

1.6.19.  301        ≠a 13 v. : ≠b ill. ; ≠c 25 cm.              _____

1.6.20.   600 20      ≠a Babin, Lisa B. ≠q (Lisa Beth)                    _____

1.6.21.   650 10      ≠a Basketball ≠x History.                          _____

1.6.22.   650 0       ≠a Indiana ≠x Description and travel.             _____

1.6.23.   610 20      ≠a Art for New Artists Conference.                _____

1.6.24.   651  0      ≠x Alaska ≠x Politics and government.             _____

1.6.25.   650  0      ≠a Automobiles ≠y Maintenance and repair.        _____

1.6.26.   651 00      ≠a Bible ≠v Commentaries.                         _____

1.6.27.   611 20      ≠a International Film Festival ≠p (1996)          _____

1.6.28.   600 20      ≠a Star (Actress)                                 _____

1.6.29.   653 07      ≠a Mystery fiction.                               _____

1.6.30.   650 0       ≠y Twentieth century.                            _____

1.6.31.   651 20      ≠a Chicago Bulls.                                 _____

1.6.32.   630 00      ≠t Bible. ≠p O.T. ≠p Psalms ≠v Commentaries.     _____

## Multiple Errors, Exercise Set 1

Find all the errors on each line. Circle them, then write the correct form above the error. There may be one or more errors per line.

1.6.33    100 1       ≠a Smith-Rosen, G. N. ≠p (Guy Ngo)

1.6.34.   110 2       ≠a Many (La.). ≠c Mayor.

1.6.35.   100 1       ≠q Smith, John Bob, ≠y 1901-1946.

1.6.36.   111 1       ≠a Golf days ≠n (10th : ≠d 1990 ; ≠c Many (La.)

1.6.37.   110 2       ≠a Louisiana. ≠a Office of Marine Fisheries.

1.6.38    245 04      ≠a The tale of two kitties / ≠c by Mama Cat.

1.6.39.   245 00      ≠b Dogs : ≠b a long tale / ≠c compiled by John Reeder.

1.6.40.   240 10      ≠a The sound and the fury / ≠b Ralph Nader.

1.6.41.   245 15      ≠a Les miserables / ≠c illustrated by Pablo Picasso.

1.6.42.   246 14      ≠a The soccer defeat : ≠b by the Boston Jets.

1.6.43.   260 0       ≠a New York : ≠b Milwaukee, ≠b c1946, ≠c 1982.

| | | |
|---|---|---|
| 1.6.44. | 261 | ≠a Many ; ≠a Shreveport ; ≠a Reeves, ≠a c1996. |
| 1.6.45. | 260 | New York : ≠b Viking, ≠b 1693. |
| 1.6.46. | 260 | ≠a Viking Press : ≠b New York ; ≠c 28 cm. |
| 1.6.47. | 260 | ≠x Baton Rouge : ≠a Ferguson Frolics, ≠y c1992. |
| 1.6.48. | 300 1 | ≠a 2 v. ; ≠a ill., maps, ports. ; ≠b 8 in. |
| 1.6.49. | 301 | ≠a x, 145, vi, 632, ix, 15 p. ; ≠b 22 cm. |
| 1.6.50. | 300 | ≠a 92 p. : ≠b col. ill., facsims. ; ≠z 28 x 22 cm. |
| 1.6.51. | 300 | ≠a [S.l.] : ≠b [s.n.], ≠c [1995]. |
| 1.6.52. | 600 10 | ≠a Smith, J. B. ≠x (John Bob), ≠y 1952- |
| 1.6.53. | 610 10 | ≠a Colorado Rodeo Association. |
| 1.6.54. | 611 10 | ≠a Lutcher Rodeo Days (≠a 1st : ≠d 1996 ; ≠b Lutcher, La.) |
| 1.6.55. | 650  0 | ≠a Sabine Parish (La.) |
| 1.6.56. | 651  0 | ≠a Rhode Island ≠z Description. |
| 1.6.57. | 650  0 | ≠a Cherokee Indians ≠y History, 18th century. |
| 1.6.58. | 600 00 | ≠a Jeremiah ≠x (Fictitious character) ≠x Fiction. |
| 1.6.59. | 600  0 | ≠a F'lar, ≠q of Pern, ≠c Dragonrider. |
| 1.6.60. | 651  0 | ≠a Utah ≠b Office of Tourism. |
| 1.6.61. | 600 10 | ≠a Jones family ≠x Genealogy. |
| 1.6.62. | 600 20 | ≠a Smith, Robbie, ≠x Biography. |
| 1.6.63. | 610 20 | ≠a Baton Rouge, Lousiana : ≠b Mayor. |
| 1.6.64. | 630 00 | ≠t Bible, N.T., Matthew. |

The number of errors in each record is given in parentheses at the top of the record. Find them and circle them. The errors may be in spelling, tags, indicators, subfields, punctuation, etc.

### 1.6.65. (12)

| | | |
|---|---|---|
| 100 1 | | ≠a Smith, James D., ≠c 1956- |
| 245 14 | | ≠a Dogs of the world / ≠c by Jim Smith, Jr. |

| 250 | ≠a First edition. |
|---|---|
| 260 | ≠a N.Y. : ≠bViking Press, ≠c1995. |
| 300 | ≠a ix, 256 p. ; ≠c col. ill., ≠c c1995. |
| 440  0 | ≠t Animals of the world. |
| 500 | ≠a Includes Index. |
| 650  0 | ≠a Dogs ≠z Encyclopedias. |

## 1.6.66 (12)

| 110 2 | ≠a Louisiana. ≠p State Records Office. |
|---|---|
| 240 10 | ≠a Registry of state lands : ≠c Louisiana State Records Office. |
| 250 | ≠a 1996 ed. |
| 260 | ≠a Baton Rouge : ≠c The Office, ≠b 1996. |
| 300 | ≠a 1 v. (various pagings) ; ≠b 28 cm. |
| 500 | ≠a Cover title. |
| 504 | ≠c Includes index. |
| 651  0 | ≠a Louisiana ≠x Registers. |
| 650  0 | ≠a Land use ≠x Louisiana. |
| 710 2 | ≠a Louisiana. ≠b State Records Office. |

## 1.6.67 (19)

| 110 1 | ≠c Robb, Randall R. |
|---|---|
| 245 04 | The archer looses an arrow : ≠c by Randall R. Robb and Sturgis S. Stubbs. |
| 246 30 | ≠i Title on spine :  ≠a Into the air. |
| 250 | ≠1 st ed. |
| 260 | ≠p New York, N.Y. :  ≠b Archery International; ≠c c2003. |
| 300 | ≠a 540 p. ; ≠c 18 cm. |
| 440  0 | ≠t Soldiery |

650 0          ≠a Horror stories.

651 0          ≠b Medieval fiction.

700 2          ≠a Stubbs, Sturgis S.

## 1.6.68. (22)

110 2          ≠a Wisconsin Library of the Arts.

245 14        ≠t Inventory control at the Library of the Arts : ≠c a manual of procedures / ≠b by the staff of the Wisconsin Library of the Arts.

260             ≠a Madison, Wisc. : ≠b Library of the Arts, ≠c 2040.

300 00        ≠a 25 l. : ≠b ill. ; ≠b 11 in.

500 00        ≠a Includes index and bibliography.

650 00        ≠a Wisconsin. ≠b Library of the Arts ≠x Handbooks, manuals, etc.

650 00        ≠a Art. ≠x Preservation.

650 10        ≠x Books ≠x Repair.

710 2          ≠a Wisconsin Library of the Arts.

## 1.6.69 (13)

100 2          ≠a Michigan ≠b Dept. of Highways.

245 10        ≠a Michigan highways.

250             A Lansin (Mich.) : ≠b Dept. of Highways, ≠c 1852 -

300             ≠v v. : b ill., maps ; c 28 cm.

321             ≠a Annual

362 0          ≠a Vol. 1, no. 1- (September 1852)-

500             ≠q Title from cover.

650 0          ≠x Michigan ≠x Periodicals.

## 1.6.70 (11)

110 2          ≠x Philadelphia (Pa.). ≠p City Council.

246 10        ≠a The early history of Philadelphia : ≠b from its founding to 1900.

250             ≠a * ed.

260            ≠a Philadelphia, Pa. : ≠b City Council, ≠c 1925.

300            ≠a xix, 312 p., 16 pages of plates : ≠b ill., maps, ports. ; ≠c 28 cm.

650  0        ≠b Philadelphia, Pennsylvania ≠x History and description.

## 1.6.71 (16)

245 10        ≠q Milne, A. G. ≠q Albert George.

245 10        ≠a The plane in Spane mainly falls ; ≠c A.G. Milne.

251           ≠a 16th edition

260           ≠a Little House Press, ≠d c1992.

300           ≠a xxxviii, 24 pages : ≠c ill., maps ; ≠c c1992.

651  1        ≠a Aircraft ≠x Spain.

## 1.6.72 (17)

110  0        ≠a Gargantua, Draconus.

240           ≠a My life as the Black Dragon / ≠b Draconus Gargantua.

250           ≠a Munich, Germany : ≠b c1994.

300           ≠A 365 p. ; ≠b illus., gen. tables ; 27 cm.

490 _ 0       \a My life series.

650 0 _       ≠a Gargantua, Draconius.

## 1.6.73 (19)

100 10        ≠a Chan, Lois Mai.

244 14        ≠b Dewey decimal classfication / ≠b a practical guide / ≠c Lois
              Mai Chan ... [et. al.]

255           ≠a 2nd ed. Revised

266           ≠a Albany : ≠b Forest Press, ≠c 1996.

300           ≠A 322 p. ≠b 8 ½ in.

500           ≠a Contains bibliographical references and index.

650  0        ≠a Classification, Dewey decimal.

# 2.

# *ANGLO-AMERICAN CATALOGUING RULES*

## 2nd edition, 2002 Revision

## Part I   Introduction

The *Anglo-American Cataloguing Rules*, second edition, commonly called *AACR2*, was published in 1978 and has been generally adopted by most English-speaking countries around the world. This acceptance is a result of the increasing use of networks and shared cataloging. The second edition has been translated, or is in the process of translation, into Arabic, Bahasa Malaysia, Chinese, Danish, Finnish, French, Italian, Japanese, Norwegian, Portuguese, Spanish, Swedish, Turkish, and Urdu. In 1988 a revision, usually called *AACR2R*, was published, and updates to the revision have been issued periodically. In 2002 a new text incorporating these updates was published. With this workbook you should use the 2002 text and any additional revisions that have been issued.

These cataloging rules were designed to cover the description and access points of all materials commonly collected at the present time. The first edition of *AACR* (published in 1967) was issued in two editions, a British text and a North American text. The second edition (1978) reconciled the British and North American texts as to style and spellings. Where Webster's *New International Dictionary*, the authority used for this edition, permitted an alternative British spelling (catalogue, centre), it has been used. Where the American usage is the only one specified, the American term is used.

Part I of *AACR2R* deals with the provision of information describing the item being cataloged, and Part II deals with the determination and establishment of headings (or access points) under which the descriptive information is to be presented to catalog users. The rules proceed from the general to the specific.

Read rules 0.1–0.29 in *AACR2R*, then complete the following exercises.

# 2.1. *AACR2R* Areas Exercises

Use the Contents pages in *AACR2R* to answer the questions. Give the area number for each specified type of information. Use the format *x.—* for your answer.

*Example:*

*Facsimiles, photocopies, and other reproductions*      <u>*x.11*</u>

2.1.1.    Title and statement of responsibility      _____

2.1.2.    Publication, distribution, etc.      _____

2.1.3.    Note area      _____

2.1.4.    Standard number and terms of availability area      _____

2.1.5.    General rules      _____

2.1.6.    Edition area      _____

2.1.7.    Supplementary items      _____

2.1.8.    Physical description area      _____

2.1.9.    Material (or type of publication) specific details area      _____

2.1.10.    Series area      _____

2.1.11.    Items made up of several types of material      _____

2.1.12.    Facsimiles, photocopies, and other reproductions      _____

Write the title of each area, and the type of format each one represents.

*Example:*

*4.4*    <u>*Manuscripts ; Publication, distribution, etc., area*</u>

2.1.13.    1.2    _____

2.1.14.    3.4    _____

2.1.15.    9.1    _____

2.1.16.    10.0    _____

2.1.17.    6.3    _____

2.1.18.    8.5    _____

2.1.19.    2.6    _____

2.1.20.    5.8    _____

2.1.21.    4.7    _____

2.1.22.  11.5 _____

2.1.23  7.9 _____

## 2.2.  *AACR2R* General Exercise

Use the frontmatter and the introductions to the various chapters in Parts I and II to answer the following questions.

2.2.1.  Who was the editor of *Anglo-American Cataloguing Rules,* 2nd edition, 1978?

2.2.2.  Are British terms of honor added to personal name entries?

2.2.3.  Which rule covers the chief source of information? Use the format (x. -- ).

2.2.4.  Which rule gives information on levels of detail in description? Use the format (x. -- ).

2.2.5.  Which rule gives information on punctuation? Use the format (x. -- ).

2.2.6.  How do I identify a transcription that contains an inaccuracy or a misspelled word?

2.2.7.  Which rule tells me so? Use the format (x. -- ).

2.2.8.  Which rule tells me how to deal with multipart items? Use the format (x. -- ).

2.2.9.  Which rule tells me how to organize the description of a work I am cataloging?

2.2.10.   Should libraries always use uniform titles in cataloging? Which rule tells me this?

2.2.11.   Do I transcribe uniform titles from a nonroman script into a roman script, or leave in a nonroman script? Which rule tells me this?

2.2.12.   Which rule tells me about the use of initial articles in uniform titles?

2.2.13.   Does *AACR2R* tell me about assigning subject headings?

2.2.14.   Which rule gives the list of general material designations (GMDs)?

2.2.15.   Are general material designations usually used with books?

2.2.16.   What is the authority used for those matters of style not covered by the rules? Which rule tells me this?

2.2.17.   Do all the examples in *AACR2R* follow all the rules? Which rule tells me this?

2.2.18.   Where would I go to find corrections, additions, or interpretations of the rules in *AACR2R*?

2.2.19.   Does *AACR2R* apply to manual or automated library catalogs, or both? Why?

2.2.20.   What does the word *prominently* mean when used in *AACR2R*? Which rule gives me this definition?

2.2.21.   Does Chapter 23 apply to both geographic entities and corporate bodies?

2.2.22.   Do you always have to make additions to personal names, such as birth and death dates, fuller forms of the name, or distinguishing phrases?

2.2.23.   Will every chapter have specific rules for everything? If not, what do I do?

2.2.24.   Is there a rule telling when you can use a corporate body as main entry? If so, which one?

# 2.3.   *AACR2R*, Part I Exercise

Use Chapter 2, "Books, Pamphlets, and Printed Sheets" to answer the following questions.

2.3.1.   What is the chief source of information for printed monographs?

2.3.2.   What do you use if there is no title page?

2.3.3.   What does *prescribed source of information* mean?

2.3.4.   Are you given specific rules for inscribing inaccuracies in a bibliographic record for a book?

2.3.5.   Are most statements used in punctuation given in terms following or preceding the various types of information?

2.3.6.   In what type of materials is the colophon considered the chief source of information?

2.3.7.   What is the prescribed source of information for the physical description of an item?

2.3.8.   For which 2.0x rules would you go to Chapter 1?

# Part II    Introduction

Part II of the *Anglo-American Cataloguing Rules*, 2002 edition, contains specific information on choice of access points, headings, uniform titles, and references. These sections will help you learn to create headings and uniform titles in the proper format.

The rules deal with the choice of access points for main and added entries, form of personal and corporate name headings, geographic entries, uniform titles, and references. The chapter on references will apply to the authority control section as well, as it deals with *See, See Also,* and explanatory references. As in Part 1, general rules precede special rules, and general rules apply where no specific rules exist.

Read the introductions (Rules 20.1–20.4, 21.0, 23.1, and 25.1) for more information on these topics.

# 2.4.    Personal Names (Chapter 22) Exercise

The following names have been found on items being cataloged by your library. Formulate them correctly according to *AACR2R* and give the rule you used as a guide.

2.4.1.   Miss Read, pseudonym of Agnes Marie Saint.

*AACR2R* rule: _____

_____

2.4.2.   By Grandfather Fortnight.

*AACR2R* rule: _____

_____

2.4.3.    By Uncle Sam.

*AACR2R* rule: _____

_____

2.4.4.    Written by D. de F.

*AACR2R* rule: _____

_____

2.4.5.    By Pliny the Elder.

*AACR2R* rule: _____

_____

2.4.6.    Saint Catherine, of Genoa.

*AACR2R* rule: _____

_____

2.4.7.    Poetry by Henri Smythe-Hetherington.

*AACR2R* rule: _____

_____

2.4.8.    Story by Marie Antoinette, queen consort of Louis XVI of France.

*AACR2R* rule: _____

_____

2.4.9.    The story of Marsilius who lived in Padua ca. 1275-1342, in his own words.

*AACR2R* rule: _____

_____

2.4.10.    The greatest poet who ever lived: Baron George Gordon Byron.

*AACR2R* rule: _____

_____

2.4.11.    By Marcus Tullius Cicero.

*AACR2R* rule: _____

_____

2.4.12.    Maria Tall Chief.

*AACR2R* rule: _____

_____

2.4.13.   Pope Leo the Thirteenth.

*AACR2R* rule: _____

_____

2.4.14.   H.G. Wells

*AACR2R* rule: _____

_____

2.4.15.   Buffalo Bob *[Television personality : Host, Howdy Doody Show]*

*AACR2R* rule: _____

_____

2.4.16.   Charles Dodgson.

*AACR2R* rule: _____

_____

2.4.17.   Barbara Michaels

*AACR2R* rule: _____

_____

2.4.18.   Hilda Doolittle

*AACR2R* rule: _____

_____

2.4.19.   Richard the Lion Heart

*AACR2R* rule: _____

_____

2.4.20.   Prince Franz Joseph, of Hohenzollern

*AACR2R* rule: _____

_____

2.4.21.   Frank MacGruff

*AACR2R* rule: _____

_____

2.4.22.   Nurse Jones

*AACR2R* rule: _____

_____

2.4.23.   John Smith *[Ship captain]*

   *AACR2R* rule: _____

---

# 2.5.   Corporate Bodies (Chapter 24), Exercise Set 1

The following corporate bodies have been found on items you are cataloging for your library collection. Use the *AACR2R* rule given and formulate the names correctly.

2.5.1.   Commission on Certification of Social Workers, Department of Health and Hospitals, Health and Social Rehabilitation Services Administration, State of Alabama.
   *AACR2R* rule: 24.19

---

2.5.2.   First Presbyterian Church, located in Boise, Idaho.

   *AACR2R* rule: 24.10B

---

2.5.3.   Commonwealth of Montana.

   *AACR2R* rule: 24.3E

---

2.5.4.   Third Governor's Conference on Mental Disabilities held in Ames, Iowa in 1957.

   *AACR2R* rule: 24.7B

---

2.5.5.   Coastal Resources Section, University of Mississippi.

   *AACR2R* rule: 24.13

---

2.5.6.   Pope Leo XIII. *[Served from 1878 to 1903; written under authority of his position within the Catholic Church]*

   *AACR2R* rule: 24.27B2

---

2.5.7.   State Committee of Louisiana's Republican Party.

   *AACR2R* rule: 24.16A

---

2.5.8.   West Baton Rouge Genealogical Society.

   *AACR2R* rule: 24.1A

---

2.5.9.   Grand Lodge of Lafayette in the Ancient and Honorable Order of Freemasons.

   *AACR2R* rule: 24.9A

---

2.5.10.  Subcommittee on the Federal-Aid Adult Daycare Program, Committee
         on Public Health of the House of Representatives, United States Government.

   *AACR2R* rule: 24.21C

---

2.5.11.  Supreme Court of the State of Nebraska.

   *AACR2R* rule: 24.23A

---

2.5.12.  Technical Services Interest Group, Maine Library Association.

   *AACR2R* rule: 24.13

---

2.5.13.  U.S.S. Kidd.

   *AACR2R* rule: 24.5C4

---

2.5.14.  University of New Orleans, Architectural Students Forum.

   *AACR2R* rule: 24.4C5

---

2.5.15.  Mississippi's Pearl River Administration.

   *AACR2R* rule: 24.18

---

2.5.16.  Society of Jesus.

   *AACR2R* rule: 24.3D1

---

2.5.17.  Western Louisiana Diocese of the Episcopal Church.

   *AACR2R* rule: 24.27C2

---

2.5.18.   Center for Louisiana Studies, University of Louisiana, Lafayette.

*AACR2R* rule: 24.12

---

2.5.19.   KEEL radio station, Shreveport, Louisiana.

*AACR2R* rule: 24.11

---

2.5.20.   Assessor of Las Vegas, New Mexico.

*AACR2R* rule: 24.20C1

---

2.5.21.   National Council of the Presbyterian Church in America.

*AACR2R* rule: 24.27A1

---

2.5.22.   Ironclad ship, the Monitor.

*AACR2R* rule: 24.4B

---

2.5.23.   A Baptist church in Brooklyn named Holy Jesus Church.

*AACR2R* rule: 24.10

---

2.5.24.   United States House of Representatives.

*AACR2R* rule:

---

2.5.25.   16th Infantry Division of the American Army.

*AACR2R* rule: 24.24A1

---

2.5.26.   Naval Air Corps of the United States.

*AACR2R* rule: 24.24A1

---

2.5.27.   Louisiana's Constitutional Convention of 1989.

*AACR2R* rule: 24.22B

---

2.5.28. Department of Revenue, State of Utah.

*AACR2R* rule: 24.18

_____

2.5.29. Fifth Rice Festival held in Cameron, Louisiana.

*AACR2R* rule: 24.8B1

_____

2.5.30. Red River Compact Administration, States of Louisiana and Texas.

*AACR2R* rule: 24.15A

_____

2.5.31. Cheniere Caminada Delta Management Program, Grand Isle, Louisiana

*AACR2R* rule: 24.17

_____

2.5.32. American embassy in Chile.

*AACR2R* rule: 24.18

_____

2.5.33. President George W. Bush.

*AACR2R* rule: 24.20B

_____

2.5.34. Kaw Valley Film & Video Inc.

*AACR2R* rule: 24.5C1

_____

# Corporate Bodies (Chapter 24), Exercise Set 2

The following names have been found on items being cataloged by your library. Formulate them correctly according to the *AACR2R* rule needed. State which rule you used to formulate the heading.

2.5.35. Mayor of South Bend, Indiana.

*AACR2R* rule: _____

_____

3.5.36.  WJBO radio station, Baton Rouge, Louisiana.

*AACR2R* rule: _____

_____

2.5.37.  Terrebonne Genealogical Society.

*AACR2R* rule: _____

_____

2.5.38.  U.S.S. Danley.

*AACR2R* rule: _____

_____

2.5.39.  Center for Wetland Resources, LSU & A&M College. *[Published in 1966.]*

*AACR2R* rule: _____

_____

2.5.40.  Pope John Paul the Second. *[Elected in 1978; written under authority of his position within the Catholic Church.]*

*AACR2R* rule: _____

_____

2.5.41.  Republican Party in Maine.

*AACR2R* rule: _____

_____

2.5.42.  State Committee of New York's Democratic Party.

*AACR2R* rule: _____

_____

2.5.43.  North Atlantic Treaty Organization.

*AACR2R* rule: _____

_____

2.5.44.  Second Governor's Conference on Physical Disabilities held in New Orleans in 1978.

*AACR2R* rule: _____

_____

2.5.45.  Special Subcommittee on the Federal-Aid Highway Program, Committee
on Public Works of the House of Representatives, United States Government.

*AACR2R* rule: _____

_____

2.5.46.  Mississippi's Environmental Protection Agency.

*AACR2R* rule: _____

_____

2.5.47.  Grand Lodge of Baton Rouge of the Ancient Order of Freemasons.

*AACR2R* rule: _____

_____

2.5.48.  LSU & A&M College, Paul M. Hebert Law Center.

*AACR2R* rule: _____

_____

2.5.49.  University of New Orleans, Tiger Tales Club.

*AACR2R* rule: _____

_____

2.5.50.  Louisiana Diocese of the Catholic Church.

*AACR2R* rule: _____

_____

2.5.51.  Second Order of St. Francis.

*AACR2R* rule: _____

_____

2.5.52.  Supreme Court of the State of Louisiana.

*AACR2R* rule: _____

_____

2.5.53.  President Kennedy.

*AACR2R* rule: _____

_____

2.5.54.  First Baptist Church, Big Wood, Louisiana.

*AACR2R* rule: _____

_____

2.5.55.   Bureau of Environmental Health, Louisiana's Department of Health and Hospitals, Health and Social Rehabilitation Services Administration.

*AACR2R* rule: _____

_____

2.5.56.   Army Air Corps of the United States.

*AACR2R* rule: _____

_____

2.5.57.   F4 Phantom.

*AACR2R* rule: _____

_____

2.5.58.   National Council of the Episcopal Church in America.

*AACR2R* rule: _____

_____

2.5.59.   United States Senate.

*AACR2R* rule: _____

_____

2.6.60.   A Catholic church in Manhattan named All Saints Church.

*AACR2R* rule: _____

_____

2.5.61.   Louisiana's Constitutional Convention of 1973.

*AACR2R* rule: _____

_____

2.5.62.   25th Infantry Division of the American Army.

*AACR2R* rule: _____

_____

2.5.63.   Third Shrimp Festival held in Houma, Louisiana.

*AACR2R* rule: _____

_____

2.5.64.   Department of Culture, Recreation and Tourism, State of Louisiana.

*AACR2R* rule: _____

_____

2.5.65.  Sabine River Compact Administration, States of Louisiana and Texas.

*AACR2R* rule: _____

_____

2.5.66.  British embassy in Mongolia.

*AACR2R* rule: _____

_____

2.5.67.  Kisatchie-Delta Regional Management Program, Alexandria, Louisiana.

*AACR2R* rule: _____

_____

2.5.68.  Coronet Film & Video Inc.

*AACR2R* rule: _____

_____

# 2.6.  Geographic Names, Exercise Set 1

The following geographic names have been found on items you are cataloging for your library. Use the *AACR2R* rule given and formulate the names correctly.

2.6.1.  Paris, France.

*AACR2R* rule: 23.4A1

_____

2.6.2.  A subdivision in Shreveport, Louisiana, called Broadmoor.

*AACR2R* rule: 23.4A1

_____

2.6.3.  Peking, China.

*AACR2R* rule: 23.2B1

_____

2.6.4.  Napoli, Italy.

*AACR2R* rule: 23.2B1

_____

2.6.5.  Ontario, Canada.

*AACR2R* rule: 23.4C1

_____

2.6.6.   Canadian city of Fort Erie.

*AACR2R* rule: 23.4C2

_____

2.6.7.   York, England.

*AACR2R* rule: 23.2B1

_____

2.6.8.   Ulaanbaatar, Mongolia.

*AACR2R* rule: 23.4E

_____

2.6.9.   The town of Linwood, Georgia, in Bartow County.

*AACR2R* rule: 23.4F1

_____

2.6.10.   The town of Linwood, Georgia in Walker County.

*AACR2R* rule: 23.4F1

_____

2.6.11.   Kansas City, Missouri.

*AACR2R* rule: 23.5A

_____

## Geographic Names, Exercise Set 2

To answer the following questions, formulate the place name according to *AACR2R* and give the rule you used to create the name. You will probably need to use a gazetteer as well as *AACR2R*.

2.6.12.   A town in Canada called Yellow Creek.

*AACR2R* rule: _____

_____

2.6.13.   Bonn, Germany.

*AACR2R* rule: _____

_____

2.6.14.   The port of Mendes in Brazil.

*AACR2R* rule: _____

_____

2.6.15.  The town of Strathaven.

*AACR2R* rule: _____

_____

2.6.16.  Queensland, Australia.

*AACR2R* rule: _____

_____

2.6.17.  Zhangmu, China.

*AACR2R* rule: _____

_____

2.6.18.  The Australian town of Alice Springs.

*AACR2R* rule: _____

_____

2.6.19.  Lhasa, Tibet.

*AACR2R* rule: _____

_____

2.6.20.  The new city of Laredo in Mexico.

*AACR2R* rule: _____

_____

2.6.21.  Bushmills, Northern Ireland.

*AACR2R* rule: _____

_____

2.6.22.  Pecos Wilderness forest area in New Mexico.

*AACR2R* rule: _____

_____

2.6.23.  Puerta Vallarta, Mexico.

*AACR2R* rule: _____

_____

2.6.24.  Omaha, Nebraska.

*AACR2R* rule: _____

_____

2.6.25.   Kathmandu, Nepal.

*AACR2R* rule: _____

_____

2.6.26.   The Welsh town of Llanelly.

*AACR2R* rule: _____

_____

2.6.27.   The town of Hidalgo in Mexico.

*AACR2R* rule: _____

_____

2.6.28.   Yukon Territory.

*AACR2R* rule: _____

_____

# 2.7.   Choice of Access Points

Access points are entries allowing access to information in a bibliographic record. Main author, title proper, uniform title, subject headings, and added entries are all examples of access points. Manual, or card catalog, systems need a main entry heading for all the works of a person to be filed together. A computer can find all the works of a person regardless of where the information is located—in a main entry, added entry, or series entry field, for example. Decisions about whether a name should be a main entry or added entry are perhaps less important for automated library systems, but contemporary practice requires that the decisions be made. This chapter will help you make decisions about those problem areas where there isn't a simple (one author, one title) choice of access points. This workbook will discuss the rules in *AACR2R* Chapter 21 dealing with text; rules dealing with nonprint materials will be discussed in the *Blitz Cataloging Workbook Series, Nonprint Materials* workbook.

## Choice of Access Points Exercise

Read the introductory rules for Chapter 21 and answer the following questions about choice of access points.

2.7.1.   Explain what the rules in this chapter determine.

2.7.2.   What determines the access points for the item being cataloged?

2.7.3.   What four terms can be appended to an added entry heading for a person?

2.7.4.   Are these terms noted in full, or abbreviated?

2.7.5.   Are these the only terms which can be added?

2.7.6.   Define *personal author*.

2.7.7.   Which rule defines the use of a corporate body as main entry?

2.7.8.   Define *emanate* as used in Rule 21.1B2.

2.7.9.   What should you do if you are in doubt about whether a work falls into one or more of the categories in Rule 21.1B2?

2.7.10.   What should you do if a work emanates from one or more corporate bodies and falls outside the categories given in Rule 21.1B2?

2.7.11.   Is a work ever entered under title main entry? If so, when?

2.7.12.   If a word in the title of a second edition of a work changes from "and" to "&", is it considered a new title?

2.7.13.   What should you do if you are in doubt as to whether the title has changed?

2.7.14.   Should you make a separate entry for a serial when the title changes, or just note the change and use the same record?

2.7.15.   If a corporate body issuing a serial changes its name, but the serial title remains the same, should you make a new record, or just note the change and use the same record?

2.7.16.   How would an official communication from a head of state be entered?

2.7.17.   How would a presidential inaugural address be entered?

2.7.18.   How should you enter a work whose identification of authorship consists of symbols ?

2.7.19.   Define *works of shared responsibility.*

2.7.20.   When should you make a title main entry even if the item being cataloged has authors?

2.7.21.   In the case of question 20, how many of the authors are given in the statement of responsibility? How many of these authors are traced as added entries?

2.7.22.   In a work of joint authorship of two persons, which is given as the main entry?

2.7.23.   If the names of joint authors appear in different order on the first and second editions of a work, how are the headings given for each work?

2.7.24.   Whose name is used as main entry when two or more persons collaborate and use a single pseudonym?

2.7.25.   What would be the main entry of a work that is a modification of another work?

2.7.26.   What would be the main entry of a work that is an abridgement or rearrangement of another work?

2.7.27.   What would be the main entry of a paraphrase, rewriting, adaptation for children, or version in a different literary form?

2.7.28.   What would be the main entry for a translation of a work?

2.7.29.   What should you do in any of the cases in 2.7.26, 2.7.27, 2.7.28, or 2.7.29 if you are in doubt?

2.7.30.   Why are added entries necessary?

2.7.31.   What types of information can be found in added entries?

2.7.32.   Must a person or corporate body be named in the descriptive part of a bibliographic record before being included as an added entry?

2.7.33.   Must all persons or corporate bodies named in the descriptive part of a bibliographic record be put in added entries?

2.7.34.   Should all items containing several named works (a collection of stories, a sound recording, or multiple plays, for example) have analytical entries?

2.7.35.   Are the legislative enactments and decrees of a political jurisdiction, and the decrees of a chief executive having the force of law, ever entered under personal name main entry?

# 2.8.   Uniform Titles

A uniform title brings together all catalog entries for a work that appears under various titles in different editions, translations, adaptations, or mediums of expression. A uniform title also correctly identifies a work when the title being cataloged is different from the title by which a work is known.

Use of uniform titles is optional; although the rules in *AACR2R* are stated as instructions, their application in any particular library depends on the policy of the library. Use of uniform titles can vary from one library to another and can even vary within a single library.

# Uniform Titles Exercise

Answer the following questions about uniform titles.

2.8.1.   How is the uniform title differentiated from the main title on a catalog card?

2.8.2.   How is the uniform title differentiated from the main title in an automated system?

2.8.3.   Does a uniform title used as a main entry heading include square brackets?

2.8.4.   How should you transcribe a uniform title that is written in nonroman script?

2.8.5   If a work is published simultaneously in the same language but with different titles, which title should be used?

2.8.6.   What is the order of preference in languages for works published simultaneously in different languages and under different titles, none of which is known to be the original language or title?

2.8.7.   If there is no title in any of the languages in the table of preference, which title would you use?

2.8.8.   If the library receives only one edition of the work referred to in questions 2.8.6 and 2.8.7, do you need to use a uniform title?

2.8.9.    If a work was originally written in classical Greek, what would you use for the uniform title?

2.8.10.   How would you distinguish between a person or corporate body and an identical uniform title being used as a heading or reference? *[Example: Charlemagne]*

2.8.11.   How would you distinguish between two identical titles which refer to different works?

2.8.12.   Where would I indicate that the item being cataloged is in a different language from the original?

2.8.13.   Would I do the same thing for a motion picture with subtitles in a different language?

2.8.14.   How would you indicate that the language of the item is an early form of a modern language?

2.8.15.   How would you indicate that the item being cataloged is in two languages, one of them the original language?

2.8.16.   What would you do if neither of the languages is the original language?

2.8.17.   What would you do if there are three languages in the work being cataloged?

2.8.18.   How would you indicate that only part of a work, unnumbered or nonconsecutively numbered, is the item being cataloged?

2.8.19.   What uniform title would I use for an item consisting of the complete works of a person?

2.8.20.   What uniform title would I use for an item consisting of more than three, but not all, works of a person?

2.8.21.   What uniform title would I use for an item consisting of the complete works of a person in one particular form?

2.8.22.   What if none of the above is appropriate?

2.8.23.   What would you use for a uniform title for a complete or partial collection of legislative enactments of a jurisdiction?

2.8.24.   What would you use for a uniform title for a single legislative enactment?

2.8.25.   What would you use for a uniform title for several different laws with the same title enacted by the same jurisdiction?

2.8.26.   What would you use for a uniform title for a collection of treaties between two given parties?

2.8.27.   What if the collection of treaties was between one party and several other parties?

2.8.28.   What would you use for a uniform title for a sacred scripture?

2.8.29.   What is the sequence in which specific parts of the Bible would be given in a uniform heading?

2.8.30.   What would the uniform title be for a group of books of the Bible?

2.8.31.   What is the uniform title for the Apocrypha?

2.8.32.   What is the uniform title for a single selection commonly identified by its own title rather than its designation as part of the Bible, for example, The Lord's Prayer?

2.8.33.   If an item consists of two Biblical selections encompassed by two uniform titles, do you use both uniform titles?

2.8.34.   What is the order for additions to uniform titles for language, date, version, and so on?

2.8.35.   What is the uniform title for a particular order or a tractate or treatise of the Talmud?

2.8.36.   What reference authority would you consult for the form of the name a particular order or tractate of the Mishnah or Tosefta?

2.8.37.   How would you enter one of the four standard collections of Vedas?

# 3.

# AUTHORITY CONTROL

Authority files represent records of decisions made about the manner in which rules have been interpreted. An authority file serves two principal purposes for the cataloger: It is a reference to which one turns to discover whether a precedent exists for a particular heading, and it provides guidance, either from context or by example, for the creation of a new heading. Authority files provide a logical organization of related topics and specific and direct access to a known topic through a single search.

If a heading is not to be used in more than one record, maintaining it in an authority file serves little purpose. One must, therefore, make a decision to authorize all headings on the premise that they will be used again, or wait until the second time a particular heading is used in a bibliographic record to do the authority work. The second option entails checking your bibliographic files for every heading, then your authority files to see if you've already created it, then either creating it or not. It seems that the first choice is less work!

Although most librarians agree that authority control is a very important element of any catalog, the time and cost required to maintain an authority file often cause it to be a low priority. Yet it is essential if the catalog is to truly serve the needs of its users. Efficient searching by author and subject is impossible if headings are inconsistent and cross-references are not available. If, for instance, some bibliographic records use Mark Twain and others use Samuel Langhorne Clemens, if some use Moss—Louisiana and some use Spanish moss, if some use Elephants and others use Pachyderms, if some use Neftali Reyes and others use Pablo Neruda, a search will retrieve only part of the library's holdings. A properly maintained authority file provides a consistent system of *See From* and *See Also* references that will result in more productive search results.

Authority control identifies the established form for headings for persons, corporate bodies, geographical names, uniform titles, series titles, subject headings of all types including topical, and any combination of these. It provides the reasons for the particular heading chosen and for alternate forms of the heading, terms used previously, and broader, narrower, and/or related terms. Uniform headings (not uniform titles) provide an efficient means of finding all works for a person, a corporate body, and so forth. They allow patrons to find all items by or about a given author or subject without having to guess how the term will be entered. This also entails background work by the cataloger, who uses an established authority file for headings, such as *Library of Congress Subject Headings* (*LCSH*) or the OCLC authority file database. Authority files can be found in machine-readable form in an integrated library system or in a separate manual card file. Both formats are discussed in this section.

The authority database is rarely available to the public. Patrons will be aware only of the *See From* and *See Also* references helping them find the correct heading.

# 3.1.   Format of Authority Records

The *Format for MARC Authority Data* contains the official rules and requirements for creating authority files.

The 008 field gives coded data that are usually repeated in text form somewhere in the authority record. Each byte in the coded string is identified as a particular piece of information, and includes type of data, romanization scheme, type of government agency, type of series, series number, record update in process code, reference evaluation code, status of authority heading code, authority reference record code, undifferentiated personal name code, encoding level, modified record code, subject heading system code, and geographic subdivision code. For actual codes and more complete information, see the *Format for MARC Authority Data.*

The established heading is the main entry of an authority record. In an automated file it is found in a 1xx field: a personal name is entered in a 100 tag, a corporate entry in a 110 tag, a topical subject heading in a 150 tag, and so on. The 1xx field is not repeatable. In a manual file, the established heading is given at the top of the card. See the examples following this section.

*See From* references are variant forms of a heading suppressed in favor of the one that has been established as the authorized form. They are found in 4xx fields. This field is repeatable. These headings may include variant spellings of the authorized term, canceled (obsolete or pre-*AACR*) terms, other forms of names, pseudonyms, transliterated terms, acronyms, fuller/lesser hierarchical names, inverted forms, and more. In a manual file, *See From* references are designated with a single "x" or with UF [*Use For*]. More than one *See From* reference may be used in any given authority record.

*See Also* terms are variant forms of a heading that may also be used. They are found in 5xx fields, also repeatable. These headings may be earlier/later forms of corporate names, broader terms, related terms, or narrower terms. When a *See Also* reference is included, it must also be created as a 1xx tag. Both headings must have individual authority records. In a manual file, *See Also* references are designated with "xx" or as BT [*Broader Term*], NT [*Narrower Term*], RT [*Related Term*], or SA [*See Also*].

Series authorities are designed to include series treatment information as well as information concerning the heading. Information about the beginning and/or ending dates of publication and/or the volume designation of a series is found in a 640 field.

The 641 field is used for numbering peculiarities. This field contains unformatted notes citing report-year coverage or irregularities and peculiarities in numbering.

Source notes are found in 670 fields. The first 670 field is always the item being cataloged, which is the source of the name or term being authorized. 670 fields can also include other authorities, such as dictionaries, gazetteers, encyclopedias, and other published reference works, used for alternate forms of the established term. Phone calls to, and letters from, the author or publisher may also be cited, as well as electronic mail messages. The 670 field is repeatable, and a record often has several sources, especially if there is a large number of *See From* and *See Also* references. When personal authors have their works translated into foreign languages, the translated forms of the name are often included as *See From* references, with the source of the translated name given in additional 670 fields. In a manual file, source notes follow the *See From* and *See Also* references.

Historical notes are used to give fuller information about previous forms of a heading such as the *AACR1* form of a name or the complex name changes typical of government agencies. These notes are found in a 667 field. Only one 667 field is used.

Epitome notes are found in a 678 field. They are used to record biographical or other information, such as profession, birthplace, or date a firm was established. This note is usually used only when converting manual files to machine-readable files. After manual files have been completed, the epitome note is incorporated into the 670 field.

Subject scope notes are used to give more information about the usage of the heading, usually referring to related or overlapping headings. These notes usually record scope notes as they appear in *LCSH*. In automated files, this note is found in a 680 field. In a manual file, the scope note follows the source notes.

The examples shown below contain a MARC record and a manual authority card.

| Rec stat: | Entered: 19950317 | | |
|---|---|---|---|
| Type: z | Upd status: a | Enc lvl: n | Source: d |
| Roman: | Ref status: a | Mod rec: | Name use: b |
| Govt agn: | Auth status: a | Subj: a | Subj use: a |
| Series: n | Auth/ref: a | Geo subd: I | Ser use: b |
| Ser num: n | Name: n | Subdiv tp: | Rules: n |

| | | |
|---|---|---|
| 040 | | ≠a LSL ≠c LSL |
| 110 | 20 | ≠a Pern Transportation Company. |
| 410 | 10 | ≠a Pern. ≠b Transportation Co. |
| 510 | 20 | ≠a Pernese Transport. |
| 670 | | ≠a Lilcamp, Jayge. Pern's premiere hauling service, 4562: p.5 (Pern Transportation Company; organized in 4537 as Pernese Transport, name changed in 4559) |

**Pern Transportation Company**

UF    Pern.  Transportation Company.
SA    Pernese Transport.

Lilcamp, Jayge. Pern's premiere hauling service, 4562: p.5 (Pern Transport Company; organized in 4537 as Pernese Transport, name changed in 4559)

Rec stat:                    Entered: 19950317

| Type: z | Upd status: a | Enc lvl: n | Source: d |
|---|---|---|---|
| Roman: | Ref status: a | Mod rec: | Name use: b |
| Govt agn: | Auth status: a | Subj: a | Subj use: a |
| Series: n | Auth/ref: a | Geo subd: I | Ser use: b |
| Ser num: n | Name: n | Subdiv tp: | Rules: n |

| 040 | | ≠a LSL ≠c LSL |
|---|---|---|
| 151 | 0 | ≠a French Quarter (New Orleans, La.) |
| 451 | 0 | ≠a Vieux Carre (New Orleans, La.) |
| 551 | 0 | ≠a Ferguson, G. New Orleans French Quarter, 2002: ≠b (French Quarter) |
| 670 | | ≠a Smith, James John. History of the Vieux Carre, 1993: ≠b p.1 (Vieux Carre, part of New Orleans, also called the French Quarter) |

**French Quarter (New Orleans, La.)**

UF     Vieux Carre (New Orleans, La.)
BT     New Orleans (La.)

Ferguson, G. History of the French Quarter, 2002: (French Quarter)
Smith, James John. History of the Vieux Carre, 1993: (Vieux Carre, part of New Orleans, also called the French Quarter)

| Rec stat: | Entered: 19950317 | | |
|---|---|---|---|
| Type: z | Upd status: a | Enc lvl: n | Source: d |
| Roman: | Ref status: a | Mod rec: | Name use: a |
| Govt agn: | Auth status: a | Subj: a | Subj use: a |
| Series: n | Auth/ref: a | Geo subd: n | Ser use: b |
| Ser num: n | Name: n | Subdiv tp: | Rules: c |

| 040 | | ≠a LSL ≠c LSL |
|---|---|---|
| 151 | 0 | ≠a Mongolia. |
| 451 | 0 | ≠a MNR. |
| 451 | 0 | ≠a Mongolia People's Republic. |
| 451 | 0 | ≠a Mongol Uls. |
| 451 | 0 | ≠a Bugd Nayramdah Mngol Ard Uls. |
| 451 | 0 | ≠a Outer Mongolia. |
| 451 | 0 | ≠a Mongolia, Outer. |
| 551 | 0 | ≠a Inner Mongolia (China) |

**Mongolia**

      UF     MNR
                Mongolia People's Republic
                Mongol Uls
                Bugd Nayramdah Mngol Ard Uls
                Outer Mongolia
                Mongolia, Outer
      RT     Inner Mongolia (China)

Rec stat:                Entered: 19950317

| Type: z | Upd status: a | Enc lvl: n | Source: d |
|---|---|---|---|
| Roman: | Ref status: a | Mod rec: | Name use: a |
| Govt agn: | Auth status: a | Subj: a | Subj use: a |
| Series: n | Auth/ref: a | Geo subd: n | Ser use: b |
| Ser num: n | Name: n | Subdiv tp: | Rules: c |

| 040 | | ≠a LSL ≠c LSL |
|---|---|---|
| 130 | 00 | ≠a Bible. ≠p N.T. ≠p John. |
| 430 | 00 | ≠a Bible. ≠p John. |
| 430 | 00 | ≠a John (Book of the New Testament) |

**Bible.  N.T.  John.**

> UF      Bible.  John.
> John (Book of the New Testament)

Rec stat:                  Entered: 19950317

| | | | |
|---|---|---|---|
| Type: z | Upd status: a | Enc lvl: n | Source: d |
| Roman: | Ref status: a | Mod rec: | Name use: a |
| Govt agn: | Auth status: a | Subj: a | Subj use: a |
| Series: n | Auth/ref: a | Geo subd: n | Ser use: b |
| Ser num: n | Name: n | Subdiv tp: | Rules: c |

| | | |
|---|---|---|
| 040 | | ≠a DLC ≠c DLC ≠d DLC |
| 100 | 0 | ≠a John, ≠c the Apostle, Saint. |
| 400 | 0 | ≠a Jean, ≠c aptre, Saint. |
| 400 | 0 | ≠a John, ≠c Saint, apostle. |
| 500 | 0 | ≠a Beloved Disciple. |
| 670 | | ≠a Hieronymus. Lives of Matthew, Mark, Luke and John, c1896. |
| 670 | | ≠a Avril, M. Saint-Jean, aptre de la Sainte Eucharistie, 1982: ≠b t.p. p.(Saint-Jean, aptre) |
| 670 | | ≠a Grassi, J.A. The secret identity of the Beloved Disciple, 1990, c1989: ≠b CIP galley (Beloved Disciple, purported author of Gospel of John; traditionally identified with John the Apostle, but author disagrees) |

---

**John, the Apostle, Saint**

| | |
|---|---|
| UF | Jean, aptre, Saint |
| | John, Saint, apostle |
| RT | Beloved Disciple |

Hieronymus. Lives of Matthew, Mark, Luke and John, c1896.
   Avril, M. Saint-Jean, aptre de la Sainte Eucharistie, 1982: t.p.  (Saint-Jean, aptre)
   Grassi, J.A. The secret identity of the Beloved Disciple, 1990: CIP galley
(Beloved Disciple, purported author of Gospel of John; traditionally identified with John
the Apostle, but author disagrees)

# 3.2.   References

The examples below are a guide to be used to complete the exercises that follow them. They contain an abbreviated MARC format followed by a brief manual form. The exercises are to be completed using both manual and MARC formats.

**Personal names, *See From* references**

1.   To the established name from another form of the name

   100   1   Smith, J. R.  ≠q (John Robert)
   400   1   Smith, John Robert.

   Smith, J. R. (John Robert)
       UF Smith, John Robert.


2.   To established name from married/maiden name

   100   1   Smith, Mary Ann Harris.
   400   1   Harris, Mary Ann.

   Smith, Mary Ann Harris.
       UF Harris, Mary Ann.


3.   To/from established name from/to a pseudonym, where only one is established

   100   1   Twain, Mark.
   400   1   Clemens, Samuel Langhorne.

   Twain, Mark.
       UF Clemens, Samuel Langhorne.


4.   To established compound-surname from other forms

   100   1   Garcia Lorca, Carlos.
   400   1   Lorca, Carlos Garcia.

   Garcia Lorca, Carlos.
       UF Lorca, Carlos Garcia.


5.   To established name from different forms of transliteration

   100   1   Evtushenko, Evgenii.
   400   1   Yevtushenko, Yevgenii.

   Evtushenko, Evgenii.
       UF Yevtushenko, Yevgenii.

**Personal names**, *See Also* **references**

(Used primarily when an author has established more than one persona and uses them in authoring various types or genres of material.)

1.   To pseudonyms from real name and/or other pseudonyms

    100   1   Mertz, Barbara.

    500   1   Michaels, Barbara.

    500   1   Peters, Elizabeth.

Mertz, Barbara.
    SA Michaels, Barbara.
    SA Peters, Elizabeth.

**Corporate names**, *See From* **references**

1.   To established name from acronyms

    110   2   Joint Council on Cataloging.

    410   2   JCC.

    410   2   J.C.C.

Joint Council on Cataloging.
    UF JCC.
    UF J.C.C.

2.   To established name from fuller hierarchical name

    110   1   Louisiana. ≠b Office of State Parks.

    410   1   Louisiana. ≠b Department of Culture, Recreation and Tourism. ≠b Office of State Parks.

Louisiana. Office of State Parks.
    UF Louisiana. Department of Culture, Recreation and Tourism. Office of State Parks.

3.   To established form from shorter form

    110   1   New Jersey. ≠b Department of Education. ≠b Music Section.

    410   1   New Jersey. ≠b Music Section.

New Jersey. Department of Education. Music Section.
    UF New Jersey. Music Section.

4.  To established form from unauthorized form which may be frequently found in publications

    110　1　　New Mexico. ≠b Office of State Fire Marshal.

    410　1　　New Mexico. ≠b State Fire Marshal.

    New Mexico. Office of State Fire Marshal.
    　　UF New Mexico. State Fire Marshal.

5.  To established form from inverted form, to facilitate searching

    110　1　　Rhode Island. ≠b Office of State Inspector General.

    410　1　　Rhode Island. ≠b State Inspector General, Office of.

    Rhode Island. Office of State Inspector General.
    　　UF Rhode Island. State Inspector General, Office of.

### Corporate names, *See Also* references

(Used especially with those government agencies whose names have changed through reorganization, although private industry is not immune from this, either. Some governmental bodies have gone through a succession of name changes and will therefore have several *See Also* references to reflect this history.)

1.  To later form from earlier form of name

    110　2　　State Library of Louisiana.

    510　2　　Louisiana State Library.

    State Library of Louisiana.
    　　SA Louisiana State Library.

2.  To earlier form from later form of name

    110　2　　Louisiana State Library.

    510　2　　State Library of Louisiana.

    Louisiana State Library.
    　　SA State Library of Louisiana.

### Subject headings, *See From* references

(Makes your catalog much more user-friendly. Points the way from an unused term, a canceled heading, or a different spelling; may turn frustration into smiles. These headings are also classed as *Use For* headings in current *LCSH* volumes.)

1. To established form from former headings that are obsolete

   150   African Americans.
   450   Afro-Americans.

   African Americans.
       UF Afro-Americans.

2. To established form from an unused heading

   150   Teenagers.
   450   Adolescents.

   Teenagers.
       UF Adolescents.

3. To established form from different spelling

   150   Teenagers.
   450   Teen-agers.

   Teenagers.
       UF Teen-agers.

**Subject headings,** *See Also* **references**

(Help point the user to other terms that may be helpful in a search.)

1. To established form from broader terms

   150   Tigers.
   550   Mammals.

   Tigers.
       BT Mammals.

2. To established form from narrower terms

   150   Iris.
   550   Louisiana iris.

   Iris.
       NT Louisiana iris.

3. To established form from another similar topic

   150   Underpasses.
   550   Subways.

   Underpasses.
       SA Subways.

**Geographical names,** *See From* **references**

1.  To established form from non-authorized form

    151  Latin America.
    451  Spanish America.

    Latin America.
        UF Spanish America.


2.  To established form from earlier name

    151  Russia, Northern
    451  Soviet Union, Northern.

    Russia, Northern.
        UF Soviet Union, Northern.


3.  To established form from abbreviation

    151  Saint Helens, Mount (Wash.)
    451  St. Helens, Mount (Wash.)

    Saint Helens, Mount (Wash.)
        UF St. Helens, Mount (Wash.)


4.  To established form from former, unauthorized form

    151  Louisiana.
    451  Louisiane.

    Louisiana.
        UF Louisiane.


5.  To established form from non-ISBD forms that were previously used for the term

    151  Cobb County (Ga.)
    451  Cobb County, Ga.

    Cobb County (Ga.)
        UF Cobb County, Ga.

**Geographical names,** *See Also* **references**

1.  To established form from broader term

    151   French Quarter (New Orleans, La.)

    551   New Orleans (La.)

    French Quarter (New Orleans, La.)
       BT New Orleans (La.)

2.  To established form from related term

    151   New York Metropolitan Area.

    551   New York Suburban Area.

    New York Metropolitan Area.
       RT New York Suburban Area.

3.  To established form from narrower term

    151   Nigeria ≠x History.

    551   Senussite Rebellion, 1916-1918.

    Nigeria—History.
       NT Senussite Rebellion, 1916-1918.

# References Exercise

Create *See From* or *See Also* references for the following terms. Use both automated and manual forms. Use correct tagging. You may need to verify 4xx and 5xx fields by using other sources such as *LCSH*, *Sears List of Subject Headings*, *AACR2R*, gazetteers, and other reference works. The term in parentheses is the form to be provided.

**Personal names,** *See From* **references**

3.2.1.   (Another form of the name)

    100 1    Jones, Seymour R.  ≠q (Seymour Rochambaud)

    *400 1*   _____

    Jones, Seymour R. (Seymour Rochambaud)

    _____

3.2.2.    (Real name)

    100 1    Brand, Max.

---

Brand, Max

---

3.2.3.    (Single surname)

    100 1    Hendricks Boynton, Janice.

---

Hendricks Boynton, Janice

---

3.2.4.    (Maiden name)

    100 1    Brown, Katherine Rice.

---

Brown, Katherine Rice

---

## Personal names, *See Also* references

3.2.5.    (Pseudonym)

    100 1    Dodgson, Charles Lutwidge, ≠d 1832-1898.

---

Dodgson, Charles Lutwidge, ≠d 1832-1898

---

## Corporate names, *See From* references

3.2.6.    (Fuller hierarchical name)

    110 1    Louisiana. ≠b Office of State Library.

---

Louisiana. Office of State Library

---

3.2.7.   (Shorter hierarchical name)

110 1     Kentucky. ≠b Department of Education. ≠b Vocational Education Section.

---

Kentucky. Department of Education. Vocational Educational Section

---

3.2.8.   (Acronym)

110 2     Bureau of National Affairs.

---

Bureau of National Affairs

---

3.2.9.   (Inverted form)

110 1     United States. ≠b Department of the Interior.

---

United States. Department of the Interior

---

## Corporate names, *See Also* references

3.2.10.   (Later form of name)

110 2     Louisiana State University and Agricultural and Mechanical College.

---

Louisiana State University and Agricultural and Mechanical College

---

3.2.11.   (Earlier form of name)

110 2     Newcomb College.

---

Newcomb College

---

**Subject headings,** *See From* **references**

    3.2.12.  (Different spelling)

        150 0    Babysitting.

---

        Babysitting

---

    3.2.13  (Obsolete heading)

        150 0    Gay men.

---

        Gay men

---

    3.2.14  (Unused heading)

        150 0    Police.

---

        Police

---

**Subject headings,** *See Also* **references**

    3.2.15.  (Similar topic)

        150 0    Cookery, American $\neq$x Louisiana style.

---

        Cookery, American—Louisiana style

---

    3.2.16  (Narrower topic)

        150 0    Reptiles.

---

        Reptiles

---

3.2.17.   (Broader topic)

150 0      Cherokee Indians.

---

Cherokee Indians

---

3.2.18.   (Related topic)

150 0      Elevators.

---

Elevators

---

**Geographical headings,** *See From* **references**

3.2.19.   (Earlier form of the name)

151 0      Kola Peninsula (Russia)

---

Kola Peninsula (Russia)

---

3.2.20.   (Abbreviation)

151 0      Saint John the Baptist Parish (La.)

---

Saint John the Baptist Parish (La.)

---

3.2.21.   (Non-ISBD form)

151 0      Ontonagon County (Mich.)

---

Ontonagon County (Mich.)

---

3.2.22.   (Former, unauthorized form)

151 0      Pennsylvania.

---

Pennsylvania

---

**Geographical names, *See Also* references**

    3.2.23.  (Related term)

        151 0     Washington D.C. Metropolitan Area.

        Washington D.C. Metropolitan Area

    3.2.24.  (Narrower term)

        151 0     New Orleans (La.)  ≠x History.

        New Orleans (La.)—History

    3.2.25  (Broader term)

        151 0     Manhattan (New York, N.Y.)

        Manhattan (New York, N.Y.)

# 3.3.    Authority Control

## Authority Control, Exercise Set 1

Decide from the above exercises which *Use For, See Also, Narrower Terms, Broader Terms,* and *Related Terms* would be applicable, and create the appropriate authority record. Not all lines will be used on every question.

    3.3.1.   Lawnmower repairs

        Source: Ferguson, Gary. Repairing your power lawnmower, c2004

        1__ __ __      ≠a _____

        4__ __ __      ≠a _____

        4__ __ __      ≠a _____

        5__ __ __      ≠a _____

        670          ≠a _____

3.3.2.    Mount Driskoll

Source:  Lilly, Joyce. Louisiana's highest peak, c1991.

| 1_ _ _ | ≠a _____ |
| 4_ _ _ | ≠a _____ |
| 4_ _ _ | ≠a _____ |
| 5_ _ _ | ≠a _____ |
| 670 | ≠a _____ |

3.3.3.    Thomas Francis Jaques

Source:  Jaques, Thomas F. Autobiography of a State Librarian,
         c2001, Thomas F. Jaques, nickname Tom, p. ii.

| 1_ _ _ | ≠a _____ |
| 4_ _ _ | ≠a _____ |
| 4_ _ _ | ≠a _____ |
| 5_ _ _ | ≠a _____ |
| 670 | ≠a _____ |

3.3.4.    Louisiana governor's office

Source: State of the state report, 1995, 1995, (Louisiana Office of the
        Governor—t.p.)

| 1_ _ _ | ≠a _____ |
| 4_ _ _ | ≠a _____ |
| 4_ _ _ | ≠a _____ |
| 670 | ≠a _____ |

3.3.5.    Oliver, Gideon

Source: Elkins, Aaron. The dark place, 1987: (also known as Professor
        Oliver and the Skeleton Detective)

| 1_ _ _ | ≠a _____ |
| 4_ _ _ | ≠a _____ |
| 4_ _ _ | ≠a _____ |
| 4_ _ _ | ≠a _____ |
| 670 | ≠a _____ |

3.3.6. Marvin W. (Trey) Lewis, III

Source: Lewis, Marvin Wells. Indian artifacts of the Gulf Coast, c1998;
phone call to author: (generally known as Trey; he was born in 1964)

1_ _ _ ≠a _____

4_ _ _ ≠a _____

4_ _ _ ≠a _____

670 ≠a _____

# 3.4. 008 (Header) Information, Authority Control

Authority records, like bibliographic records, contain an 008 field, which consists of coded data about the record. The information, however, deals with specifics such as romanization scheme, type of series, type of government document, and whether it is a subject heading or an author heading. There are forty bytes (00–39), each with a specific meaning. The codes below will help you fill out the header for authority records and complete the given exercises.

00-05—Date entered on file. Formatted as *yymmdd* (year/year/month/month/day/day)

06—Direct or indirect geographic subdivision; indicates whether the 1xx heading may be subdivided geographically when used as a subject heading and, if so, the method of subdivision used.

    (blank)—Not geographically subdivided

    d—Subdivided geographically—direct

    i—Subdivided geographically—indirect

    n—Not applicable

07—Romanization scheme; indicates whether the 1xx field contains the romanized form of the heading and, if so, the romanization scheme used.

    a—International standard

    b—National standard

    c—National library association standard

    d—National library or bibliographic agency standard

    e—Local standard

    f— Standard of unknown origin

    g—Conventional romanization or conventional form of name in language of cataloging agency

    n—Not applicable; the 1xx heading is not romanized

08—Language of catalog; indicates whether the heading in the 1xx field and its associated reference structure are valid according to the rules used in establishing heading for English-language catalogs, French-language catalogs, or both.

> #—No information provided
>
> b—English and French
>
> e—English only
>
> f—French only

09—Kind of record; indicates whether the record represents an established or unestablished 1xx heading.

> a—Established heading
>
> b—Untraced reference; not traced as a 4xx field in any established heading record
>
> c—Traced reference; contains an unestablished heading that is traced as a 4xx field in the record
>
> d—Subdivision; unestablished heading that may be used as a subject subdivision
>
> e—Node label
>
> f—Established heading and subdivision; an established heading that may be used as a main term and as a subject subdivision
>
> g—Reference and subdivision; unestablished heading that may be used as a reference term and as a subject division

10—Descriptive cataloging rules

> a—Earlier rules; cataloging conventions used prior to *AACR1*
>
> b—*AACR1*
>
> c—*AACR2*
>
> d—*AACR2*-compatible heading
>
> n—Not applicable
>
> z—Other

11—Subject heading system/thesaurus

> a—Library of Congress Subject Headings
>
> b—LC subject headings for children's literature
>
> c—Medical Subject Headings (MeSH)
>
> d—National Agriculture Library subject authority file
>
> k—Canadian Subject Headings
>
> n—Not applicable
>
> r—Art and Architecture Thesaurus
>
> s—Sears List of Subject Headings
>
> v—Repertoire des vedettes-matiere
>
> z—Other

12—Type of series
    a—Monographic
    b—Multipart item
    c—Series-like phrase
    d—Not applicable
    z—Other

13—Numbered or unnumbered series
    a—Numbered
    b—Unnumbered
    c—Numbering varies
    n—Not applicable

14—Heading use—main or added entry
    a—Appropriate
    b—Not appropriate

15—Heading use—subject added entry
    a—Appropriate
    b—Not appropriate

16—Heading use—series added entry
    a—Appropriate
    b—Not appropriate

17—Type of subject subdivision
    a—Topical
    b—Form
    c—Chronological
    d—Geographic
    e—Language
    n—Not applicable

18–27—Undefined
    (blank) or | (fill character)

28—Type of government agency
    (blank)—Not a government agency
    a—Autonomous or semi-autonomous
    c—Multilocal
    f— Federal/national
    I— International

l—Local

m—Multistate

o—Government agency, type undetermined

s—State, provincial, etc.

u—Unknown if heading is a government agency or not

z—Other

29—Reference evaluation; indicates whether the 4xx/5xx tracing fields in a record have been evaluated for consistency with the rules used to formulate the 1xx heading.

  a—Tracings consistent with heading

  b—Tracings not necessarily consistent with heading

  n—Not applicable

30—Undefined

  (blank) or | (fill character)

31—Record update in process code

  a—Record can be used

  b—Record being updated; do not use

32—Undifferentiated personal name; indicates whether a personal name heading is used by one person or by two or more persons.

  a—Differentiated personal name

  b—Undifferentiated personal name

  n—Not applicable

33—Level of establishment

  a—Fully established

  b—Memorandum; heading is fully established but has not been used in a bibliographic record

  c—Provisional; heading cannot be formulated satisfactorily because of inadequate information

  d—Preliminary; heading taken from a bibliographic record because the bibliographic item was not available at the time the heading was established

  n—Not applicable

34–37—Undefined

  (blank) or | (fill character)

38— Modified record code

  (blank)—Not modified

  s—Shortened

  x—Missing characters

39—Cataloging source

> (Blank)—National bibliographic agency
>
> c—Cooperative cataloging program
>
> d—Other
>
> u—Unknown

## Authority Control Header, Exercise Set 1

Use the codes given above to create 008 tags (fixed field information) from the information given in each record. Use the date you create the information, in the form of *yymmdd* [year/year/month /month/day/day]; that is, August 5, 1997, would be coded 970805. Some positions in the 008 field will be blank.

3.4.1.    008    . . . . . . . . . . . . . . . . . . . . . . . . . . . . . . . . . . . . . . .

100    1    ≠a Sharp, Sam H., ≠d 1943-

400    1    ≠a Sharp, Samuel Harelson, ≠d 1943-

670         ≠a His Exercise by mail delivery, 1996: ≠b t.p. (Sam H. Sharp); p. ii (born Samuel Harelson Sharp, Jr. in 1943)

670         ≠a Letter from author: (Prefers to be known as Sam H. Sharp)

3.4.2.    008    . . . . . . . . . . . . . . . . . . . . . . . . . . . . . . . . . . . . . . .

100    1    ≠a Sharp, Sam H., ≠d 1967-

400    1    ≠a Sharp, Samuel Harelson, ≠d 1967-

670         ≠a His Programming made easy, 1998: ≠b t.p. (Sam H. Sharp, III); p. ii (born Samuel Harelson Sharp, III in 1967)

670         ≠a Letter from author: (Prefers to be known as Sam H. Sharp)

3.4.3.    008    . . . . . . . . . . . . . . . . . . . . . . . . . . . . . . . . . . . . . . .

100    1    ≠a Finley, Betty Jo.

400    0    ≠a Finley, Elizabeth Josephine.

670         ≠a Her Cataloging for demonstration libraries, 1972: ≠b t.p. (Betty Jo Finley; t.p. verso Elizabeth Josephine Finley)

670         ≠a Letter from author: (Prefers Betty Jo Finley)

3.4.4.    008    . . . . . . . . . . . . . . . . . . . . . . . . . . . . . . . . . . . . . . .

100    1    ≠a Wilde, Oscar, ≠d 1854-1900.

400    1    ≠a Wilde, Oscar Fingall O'Flahertie Wills, ≠d 1854-1900.

400    1    ≠a C. 3. 3., ≠d 1854-1900.

670         ≠a His The letters, c1962: ≠b p. 3 (b. 16 Oct. 1854; 26 Apr. 1855 christened)

| | | |
|---|---|---|
| 670 | | ≠a Montgomery Hyde, H. Oscar Wilde, c1975: ≠b p.6 (b. 16 Oct. 1854; several biogr. and encyc. articles, incl. Dict. of natl. biog., wrongly state b. 16 Oct. 1856; error seems arisen from his vanity in habitually understating his age; date of b. placed beyond doubt by his baptismal record, which is still in existence) |
| 670 | | ≠a Halkett & Laing: ≠b v.1, p. 172 (C.3.3. [Oscar Wilde]) |
| 670 | | ≠a His Children in prison... 1898 ≠b (hdg.: Wilde, Oscar, 1854-1900; variant: Oscar Fingall O'Flahertie Wills Wilde) |

3.4.5.   008   . . . . . . . . . . . . . . . . . . . . . . . . . . . . . . . . . . . . . . . .

| | | |
|---|---|---|
| 100 | 1 | ≠a Cartwright, George, ≠d 1739-1819. |
| 400 | 1 | ≠a G. C. ≠q (George Cartwright), ≠d 1739-1819. |
| 400 | 1 | ≠a C., G. ≠q (George Cartwright, ≠d 1739-1819. |
| 670 | | ≠a His A journal of transactions and events, ... 1792: ≠b t.p. (George Cartwright, Esq.) |

3.4.6.   008   . . . . . . . . . . . . . . . . . . . . . . . . . . . . . . . . . . . . . . . .

| | | |
|---|---|---|
| 110 | 2 | ≠a West Baton Rouge Parish Library. |
| 410 | 1 | ≠a West Baton Rouge Parish (La.). ≠b Library. |
| 550 | | ≠a Public libraries ≠z Louisiana ≠z Port Allen. |
| 670 | | ≠a Boyce, Judy. Three Frog Night, c1996: ≠b t.p. (West Baton Rouge Parish Library, Port Allen, Louisiana) |

3.4.7.   008   . . . . . . . . . . . . . . . . . . . . . . . . . . . . . . . . . . . . . . . .

| | | |
|---|---|---|
| 110 | 2 | ≠a Saint James Episcopal Church (Baton Rouge, La.) |
| 410 | 2 | ≠a St. James Episcopal Church (Baton Rouge, La.) |
| 410 | 1 | ≠a Baton Rouge (La.). ≠b Saint James Episcopal Church. |
| 550 | | ≠a Episcopal church ≠z Louisiana ≠z Baton Rouge. |
| 670 | | ≠a Its One hundred years at Saint James, 1995: ≠b t.p. (Saint James Episcopal Church, Baton Rouge, Louisiana) |

3.4.8.   008   . . . . . . . . . . . . . . . . . . . . . . . . . . . . . . . . . . . . . . . .

| | | |
|---|---|---|
| 110 | 2 | ≠a Columbia Pictures. |
| 410 | 2 | ≠a Columbia Pictures Industries. ≠b Columbia Pictures. |
| 670 | | ≠a Silverado [MP], 1985: ≠b credits (Columbia Pictures) |
| 670 | | ≠a LC data base, 10-9-86 ≠b (hdg.: Columbia Pictures) |
| 670 | | ≠a International motion picture almanac, 1983 ≠b (Columbia Pictures Corporation was incorporated in 1/10/24. In 12/28/68 Columbia Pictures Corporation was reorganized as Columbia Pictures Industries, Inc. with Columbia Pictures as a major division) |

3.4.9.   008   . . . . . . . . . . . . . . . . . . . . . . . . . . . . . . . .

    110   2   ≠a American Telephone and Telegraph Company.

    410   2   ≠a A.T. & T.

    410   2   ≠a Bell Telephone System.

    410   2   ≠a American Telephone & Telegraph Company.

    410   2   ≠a AT&T.

    510   2   ≠a American Bell Telephone Company.

    670   ≠a Its Annual report, 1900.

    670   ≠a Wasserman, N. From invention to innovation, c1985: ≠b CIP galley (AT & T: American Telephone and Telegraph Company)

    670   ≠a LC manual auth. cd. ≠b (hdg.: American Bell Telephone Company; organized 1880; merged 1900 in the American Telephone and Telegraph Company which had originally been formed, 1885, by the American Bell Telephone Company to build and operate its long distance system)

3.4.10   008   . . . . . . . . . . . . . . . . . . . . . . . . . . . . . . . .

    110   2   ≠a National Air and Space Museum.

    410   2   ≠a Smithsonian Institution. ≠b National Air and Space Museum.

    410   1   ≠a United States. ≠b National Air and Space Museum.

    410   2   ≠a Smithsonian Air and Space Museum.

    410   1   ≠a Washington (D.C.). ≠b National Air and Space Museum.

    410   2   ≠a Air and Space Museum (U.S.)

    510   2   ≠a National Air Museum (U.S.)

    670   ≠a Dickey, P.S. The Liberty engine, 1918-1942, 1968.

3.4.11.   008   . . . . . . . . . . . . . . . . . . . . . . . . . . . . . . . .

    150   ≠a Enriched cereal products.

    450   ≠a Cereal products, Enriched.

    450   ≠a Fortified cereal products.

    550   ≠a Cereal products.

    550   ≠a Enriched foods.

    670   ≠a Smith, Judith. Sources for fortified cereals, c1997

3.4.12.   008   . . . . . . . . . . . . . . . . . . . . . . . . . . . . . . . .

    150   ≠a Iran-Contra Affair, 1985-1990.

    450   ≠a Contra-Iran Affair, 1985-1990.

    450   ≠a Contragate, 1985-1990.

    450   ≠a Iran-Contra Arms Scandal, 1985-1990.

    450   ≠a Irangate, 1985-1990.

|     |     |
|-----|-----|
| 550 | ≠a Military assistance, American ≠z Iran. |
| 550 | ≠a Military assistance, American ≠z Nicaragua. |
| 550 | ≠a Political corruption ≠z United States. |
| 551 | ≠a United States ≠x Politics and government ≠y 1981-1989. |
| 670 | ≠a South, Olive. Oh, what tales..., 1993 |

3.4.13.   008 . . . . . . . . . . . . . . . . . . . . . . . . . . . . . . . . .

|     |     |
|-----|-----|
| 150 | ≠a Teuso languages. |
| 450 | ≠a Kuliak languages. |
| 550 | ≠a Nilo-Saharan languages. |
| 551 | ≠a Uganda ≠x Languages. |
| 670 | ≠a Tsingeng, Baharu. Aspects of the Teuso languages, c1994. |

3.4.14.   008 . . . . . . . . . . . . . . . . . . . . . . . . . . . . . . . . .

|     |     |
|-----|-----|
| 150 | ≠a Smock family. |
| 450 | ≠a Smack family. |
| 450 | ≠a Smak family. |
| 450 | ≠a Smoke family. |
| 450 | ≠a Smook family. |
| 550 | ≠a Schmucker family. |
| 670 | ≠a Smoke, Jan. Smoke, Smook, and Smack get in your eyes, c1995. |

3.4.15.   008 . . . . . . . . . . . . . . . . . . . . . . . . . . . . . . . . .

|     |     |
|-----|-----|
| 151 | ≠a Badlands Wilderness (Or.) |
| 451 | ≠a Badlands Wilderness Study Area (Or.) |
| 550 | ≠a National parks and reserves ≠z Oregon. |
| 550 | ≠a Wilderness areas ≠z Oregon. |
| 670 | ≠a Rancher, Buddy. Badlands as bad lands, c1987. |

3.4.16.   008 . . . . . . . . . . . . . . . . . . . . . . . . . . . . . . . . .

|     |     |
|-----|-----|
| 150 | ≠a Country musicians. |
| 450 | ≠a Hillbilly musicians. |
| 550 | ≠a Musicians. |
| 550 | ≠a Bluegrass musicians. |
| 550 | ≠a Gospel musicians. |
| 550 | ≠a Women country musicians. |
| 670 | ≠a Tonesing, Ada. Music awards, c1987. |

3.4.17.  008  . . . . . . . . . . . . . . . . . . . . . . . . . . . . . . . . . . . . . . . . . . .

      151  ≠a Kalamazoo (Mich.)

      451  ≠a Kalamazoo, Mich.

      670  ≠a Tucker, Dave. Life in Kalamazoo, c2003.

3.4.18.  008  . . . . . . . . . . . . . . . . . . . . . . . . . . . . . . . . . . . . . . . . . . .

      151  ≠a Misquah Hills (Minn.)

      451  ≠a Misquah Hills, Minn.

      550  ≠a Hills ≠z Minnesota.

      670  ≠a Ferguson, Terre. Hiking the Misquah Hills, c2002.

3.4.19.  008  . . . . . . . . . . . . . . . . . . . . . . . . . . . . . . . . . . . . . . . . . . .

      151  ≠a Mombasa (Kenya)

      451  ≠a Mombasa, Kenya

      670  ≠a Freyou, Denise. Festivals in Mombasa and other Kenyan towns, c2004.

3.4.20.  008  . . . . . . . . . . . . . . . . . . . . . . . . . . . . . . . . . . . . . . . . . . .

      151  ≠a Walsingham (England)

      451  ≠a Walsingham (Norfolk)

      451  ≠a Little Walsingham (England)

      670  ≠a Fisher, C. Walsingham, a place of pilgrimage..., 1983.

3.4.21.  008  . . . . . . . . . . . . . . . . . . . . . . . . . . . . . . . . . . . . . . . . . . .

      130  0  ≠a Time Life books your money matters

      410  2  ≠a Time Life Books. ≠t Time Life Books your money matters

      430  0  ≠a Your money matters (Alexandria, Va.)

      643  ≠a Alexandria, VA ≠b Time-Life

      670  ≠a Basics of investing, 1996: ≠b CIP t.p. (Time Life Books your money matters)

3.4.22.  008  . . . . . . . . . . . . . . . . . . . . . . . . . . . . . . . . . . . . . . . . . . .

      130  0  ≠a G.K. Hall large print book series

      430  0  ≠a Hall large print book series

      430  0  ≠a G.K. Hall large print series

      430  0  ≠a Boston, Mass. ≠b G.K. Hall

      670  ≠a Marshall, C. Julie, 1985, c1984: ≠b CIP t.p. verso

3.4.23.  008    . . . . . . . . . . . . . . . . . . . . . . . . . . . . . . . . . .

130   0      ≠a Social work practice with children and families

643           ≠a New York ≠b Guilford Press

670           ≠a Webb, N.B. Social work practice with children, 1996: ≠b CIP data
              sheet (Social work practice with children and families)

3.4.24.  008    . . . . . . . . . . . . . . . . . . . . . . . . . . . . . . . . . .

130   0      ≠a Social movements past and present

430   0      ≠a Social movements past & present

430   0      ≠a Twayne's social movements series

430   0      ≠a Twayne's social movements past and present

643           ≠a Boston, Mass. ≠b Twayne Publishers ≠d <1982-1991>

3.4.25.  008    . . . . . . . . . . . . . . . . . . . . . . . . . . . . . . . . . .

130   0      ≠a Bulletin (Louisiana. Dept. of Education)

410   0      ≠a Louisiana. ≠b Dept. of Education. ≠t Bulletin

410   0      ≠a Louisiana. ≠b Dept. of Education. ≠t Bulletin — Louisiana State
              Department of Education

643           ≠a Baton Rouge, LA (P.O. Box 44064, Baton Rouge, 70804) ≠b
              Printing Section, Dept. of Education.

# Authority Control Header, Exercise Set 2

You have found the following headings when cataloging items for your library. Search OCLC authority files for them and give the information requested. Some of the headings are not in the proper authorized form; some are. Note the proper authorized form where there is a discrepancy. If the heading given to you below has a subdivision after a dash, see if you can locate an authority file for the subdivision. Give the correct tags, indicators, and delimiters for each heading **as it would be added to the bibliographic record**, not the authority record. Give the Authority Record Number (ARN) for each heading and subdivision.

Use the following commands to search for specific terms:

*sca pn*    personal name headings

*sca co*    corporate name headings

*sca cn*    conference or meeting headings

*sca su*    subject headings

*sca ti*    titles

*sca sb*    subdivisions

3.4.26.  United States. Topographical Bureau

Heading:_____

ARN:_____

3.4.27.  Baton Rouge (La.)—Maps

Heading:_____

ARN:_____

3.4.28.  Smith, Joseph

Heading:_____

ARN:_____

3.4.29.  Art, American

Heading:_____

ARN:_____

3.4.30.  Topeka, KA

Heading:_____

ARN:_____

3.4.31.  Animals—Africa

Heading:_____

ARN:_____

3.4.32.  Hibernia Bank

Heading:_____

ARN:_____

3.4.33.  Alabama Museum of Natural History

Heading:_____

ARN:_____

3.4.34.  Superbowl

Heading:_____

ARN:_____

3.4.35.  Computer indexed marriage records

Heading:_____

ARN:_____

3.4.36.   President's Commission on Women

Heading:_____

ARN:_____

3.4.37.   Louisiana State University (Baton Rouge, La.). Paul M. Hebert Law Center

Heading:_____

ARN:_____

3.4.38.   Fletcher, Mary Dell

Heading:_____

ARN:_____

3.4.39.   Fishing—Humor

Heading:_____

ARN:_____

3.4.40.   Crayfish—Marketing

Heading:_____

ARN:_____

3.4.41.   Uluru (Ayers Rock) National Park

Heading:_____

ARN:_____

3.4.42.   Fantastic fiction.

Heading:_____

ARN:_____

3.4.43.   U.S. Navy—Biography

Heading:_____

ARN:_____

3.4.44.   Popular music, Country style

Heading:_____

ARN:_____

3.4.45.   Arithmetic—Study and teaching (Primary)

Heading:_____

ARN:_____

3.4.46.   China—Description and travel

Heading:_____

ARN:_____

3.4.47.   Masters Golf Tournament

Heading:_____

ARN:_____

3.4.48.   Fort Bayard (N.M.) — Maps

Heading:_____

ARN:_____

3.4.49.   Calcutta

Heading:_____

ARN:_____

3.4.50.   Marrakech

Heading:_____

ARN:_____

3.4.51.   Scenic waterways

Heading:_____

ARN:_____

3.4.52.   Forbidden City

Heading:_____

ARN:_____

3.4.53.   Alexander the Great

Heading:_____

ARN:_____

3.4.54.   Princess Diana

Heading:_____

ARN:_____

3.4.55.   Space

Heading:_____

ARN:_____

3.4.56.  Tbilisi, Republic of Georgia

Heading:_____

ARN:_____

3.4.57.  Fishing nets—Mekong River

Heading:_____

ARN:_____

3.4.58.  Swamps—Florida

Heading:_____

ARN:_____

3.4.59  Mountain climbing guides—Nepal

Heading:_____

ARN:_____

# 3.5. Authority Control Creation

Create an authority record for each of the following items. Use the information provided and, if necessary, consult *LCSH, Sears List of Subject Headings, AACR2R*, a gazetteer, or other reference works. You are given the term the way it appears on the item being cataloged, and it is not necessarily the way it is to be established, although it MAY be.

Each record must have a main entry, at least one *See From* reference or one *See Also* reference (some may have more than one of each), and at least one source note. If *See Also* references are made, another authority record for the *See Also* reference as a main heading MUST also be made.

Number each record you create with the number of the particular heading. You will have the same number of several records when you include *See Also* records.

You must also give your record an 040 tag, with subfields ≠a and ≠c. The first subfield (≠a) identifies the creator of the record. Use your initials (first, middle, last) in the ≠a. The second subfield (≠c) tells the source of the authority. If you use Library of Congress as your authority (subject or name), code the ≠c as DLC. If you use *Sears List of Subject Headings* as your authority, code the ≠c as SSH. If you use your own judgment (i.e., create the authorized heading as you think it should be), code the ≠c with your initials (first, middle, last).

Fill in the templates at the end of the list of terms with your answers. If you use a 5xx field, you must make two authority records. Put the number of the term being authorized in the space given on the template; if you have two authority records for the item, both authority records should have the same number.

**Corporate Names**

3.5.1.   Westin Photographic Company

Sources:

1. *Westin Professional Moving Pictures and Stills*, c1983 (Westin Photographic Company)

2. Smith, William Robert. *A Westin History*, c1993 (Westin Photographic Company; established in August 1901 as Westin Films; succeeded by Westin Photographs, 1918; Westin Photographic Company in 1935.) (The company began publishing in 1952.)

3.5.2.   Louisiana State Department of Education

Sources:

1. La. Bureau of Minority Education. *End-of-the-year report for minority education programs, 1984* (Louisiana Dept. Of Education; Louisiana State Dept. of Education)

2. Matt, Katherine. *Louisiana history*, 1966. (State Dept. Of Public Education)

3.5.3.   Minton-Shropshire Porcelain Co., Ltd.

Sources:

1. *Pseudo-porcelains*, 1895 (Minton-Shropshire Porcelain Company Limited)

2. William, Teal. *The history of the Minton and Shropshire Companies*, 1996 (Firm founded in 1832 as Minton-Shropshire Porcelain Company Limited; used "Minton Porcelain Company", "Shropshire Porcelain Company" and "M-SP" on various manufactures during 1835-1839; began again in 1840 using Minton-Shropshire Porcelain Co.)

3.5.4.   National Library of Medicine

Sources:

1. U.S. Congress. Senate Committee on the Judiciary. *A National Library of Medicine: hearings*, 1956. (National Library of Medicine)

2. *Centenary of Index Medicus, 1879-1979*, 1980 (U.S. Dept. Of Health and Human Services, Public Health Service, National Institutes of Health, National Library of Medicine)

3. *Index of NLM serial titles*, [1972]- (NLM)

3.5.5.   PAR

Source:

1. *A PAR report, 1951* (Public Affairs Research Council of Louisiana, inc.)

Note: Organized in 1950.

3.5.6.  St. Boudreaux County Public Library

Source:

1.  Majors, John B. *The end of the line*, c1975 (St. Boudreaux County Public Library)

3.5.7.  Our Lady of the Mountains Undergraduate Library

Sources:

1.  Marsh, Guinevere. *University of Guadalupe Libraries*, 1993 (Our Lady of the Mountains Undergraduate Library; OLM Library)

2.  Sangria, Maria. *Holdings in the OLM Library*, 1988 (OLM Library; Our Lady Undergraduate Library; Our Lady of the Mountains Undergraduate Library)

3.5.8.  US3, Irish rock group

Sources:

1.  *Cedar trees of heaven* [SR], 1984 (US3)

2.  Smith, Jim. "US 3 have made it big in the U.S.", *Newsweekly*, Aug. 15, 1997 (US3; Us Three)

## Geographic Names

3.5.9.  Bay of Cartagena in Colombia

Source:

1.  Willow,Diego. *A multisensory picture of Cartagena Bay, Colombia*, 1982 (Cartagena Bay)

3.5.10.  Khangai Mountains (Mongolia)

Source:

1.  Jeffries, P. Cycling the Khanghai on your BMW, c2002.

3.5.11.  Karana, the ancient city in Iraq

Source:

1.  Killeen, Sheila. *El Souk and Karana*, c1976 (Karana, Iraq)

3.5.12.  England's Lake District

Source:

1.  Marsh, Inde. *Touring the Lake District*, 1994.

3.5.13.  Gulf of Mexico

Source:

1.  Lockout, Clyde. *The Gulf of Mexico*, 1973.

3.5.14.   Mississippi Valley

Source:

1.  Halley, B.T. *Big Father of Waters*, 1989 (Mississippi River; Mississippi Valley)

3.5.15.   Lake Pontchartrain

Source:

1.  Jones, Billy Bob. *Lake Pontchartrain*, c1954.

3.5.16.   Middle fork of the Salmon River, Idaho

Source:

1.  Zines, Winfred. *Middle Fork of the Salmon*, c1980.

## Personal Names

3.5.17.   Mickey W

Sources:

1.  *The Autobiography of Mickey W*, 1978 (Mickey W; b. 1942, d. 1970)
2.  *Encyclopedic dictionary of African-Americans*, c1975 (Mickey W, born 1/1/42,d. 2/2/70; b. as Michael Jones; also known as Big Al Mullins)

3.5.18.   Governor Jimmie Davis

Sources:

1.  *Louisiana, here I come!* 1963 (Jimmie Davis)
2.  Davis, Jimmie. *You are my sunshine*, 1985 (James Houston Davis, b. 9/11/02; governor of Louisiana 1944-1948, 1960-1964; preferred to be known as Jimmie)

3.5.19.   John Huey

Sources:

1.  His *The extraneous murders*, 1923.
2.  *Contemptuous Authors*, v. 1195 (b. 3/29/1874, d. 8/28/1969; b. as Charles John Huey Smith). Also writes as Charles Smith.

3.5.20.   Vincent-Willem van Gogh

Sources:

1.  *Tableaux, aquarelles, dessin...* 1904 (Vincent van Gogh)
2.  *Vincent van Gogh (1853-1890)*, 1958 (Vincent-Willem van Gogh, b. 3/30/1853, d. 7/29/1890)

3.5.21.   Carolyn Lambert-Pitcherly

Sources:

1.  *First you must make the roux*, by Carolyn Lambert-Pitcherly, c1991.
2.  *Great Chefs of the South*, 1995 (Carolyn Landry Pitcherly)

3.5.22.   Susan L. Bentley
    Sources:

    1. *Avoyelles Parish, the happy parish*, by Susan L. Bentley, c1979.

    2. Lewis, M. L., III. *Coushatta and the Indians*, c1994 (Sue Bentley)

3.5.23.   Donald Henry Bartholomew
    Sources:

    1. *Don Bartholomew's Mongolia*, c1996.

    2. Phone call to author, 5/16/96: full name is Donald Henry Bartholomew; born in Ulaanbaatar, Mongolia, on 1/25/63; usage: Don Bartholomew)

3.5.24.   Mrs. Humphry Ward
    Sources:

    1. *Helbeck of Bannisdale*, 1883, by Mrs. Humphry Ward (b. Mary Augusta Arnold; in Hobart, Tasmania, in 1851)

    2. *Oxford companion to English literature*, 1985 (Mary Augusta Ward; d. 1920)

## Topical Subject Headings

3.5.25.   Coats of arms
    Source:

    1. Brault, G. J. *Early blazon*, c1972.

3.5.26.   Catahoula hounds
    Source:

    1. Jenkins, Huey. *Encyclopedia of the Catahoula hound*, c1992.

    2. Brown, W.C. *The Catahoula hog dog*, c1962.

3.5.27.   Exhaustion, Mental
    Source:

    1. Green, W.J. *Fatigue free*, c1992.

    2. Ferguson, Bobby. *How to catalog with joy*, c1999.

3.5.28.   Growing roses
    Source:

    1. Baker, M.L. *Roses and their culture*, c1991.

3.5.29.   Pedigreed Rhodesian ridgeback dogs
    Source:

    1. Linzy, J. *Rhodesian ridgeback champions, 1955-1980*, c1981.

    2. Jeffries, Prince. *Hounds of the world*, c1975.

3.5.30. Christian theology
Source:
1. Montefiore, H. *Credible Christianity*, c1994.

3.5.31. Garlands
Source:
1. Pflumm, C.C. *Hearthstrings*, c1993.

3.5.32. Painting with acrylic paints
Source:
1. Taubes, F. *Acrylic painting for the beginner*, c1971.

# TEMPLATES

No. _____
008
040          ≠a_____          ≠c_____
1_ _ _ _     ≠a_____
4_ _ _ _     ≠a_____
4_ _ _ _     ≠a_____
5_ _ _ _     ≠a_____
5_ _ _ _     ≠a_____
670          ≠a_____
670          ≠a_____

No. _____
008
040          ≠a_____          ≠c_____
1_ _ _ _     ≠a_____
4_ _ _ _     ≠a_____
4_ _ _ _     ≠a_____
5_ _ _ _     ≠a_____
5_ _ _ _     ≠a_____
670          ≠a_____
670          ≠a_____

No. _____
008
040          ≠a_____          ≠c_____
1_ _ _ _     ≠a_____
4_ _ _ _     ≠a_____
4_ _ _ _     ≠a_____
5_ _ _ _     ≠a_____
5_ _ _ _     ≠a_____
670          ≠a_____
670          ≠a_____

No. _____
008
040     ≠a_____     ≠c_____
1_ _ _ _   ≠a_____
4_ _ _ _   ≠a_____
4_ _ _ _   ≠a_____
5_ _ _ _   ≠a_____
5_ _ _ _   ≠a_____
670     ≠a_____
670     ≠a_____

No. _____
008
040     ≠a_____     ≠c_____
1_ _ _ _   ≠a_____
4_ _ _ _   ≠a_____
4_ _ _ _   ≠a_____
5_ _ _ _   ≠a_____
5_ _ _ _   ≠a_____
670     ≠a_____
670     ≠a_____

No. _____
008
040     ≠a_____     ≠c_____
1_ _ _ _   ≠a_____
4_ _ _ _   ≠a_____
4_ _ _ _   ≠a_____
5_ _ _ _   ≠a_____
5_ _ _ _   ≠a_____
670     ≠a_____
670     ≠a_____

No. _____
008
040     ≠a_____     ≠c_____
1_ _ _ _   ≠a_____
4_ _ _ _   ≠a_____
4_ _ _ _   ≠a_____
5_ _ _ _   ≠a_____
5_ _ _ _   ≠a_____
670     ≠a_____
670     ≠a_____

No. _____
008
040          ≠a_____          ≠c_____
1_ _ _ _     ≠a_____
4_ _ _ _     ≠a_____
4_ _ _ _     ≠a_____
5_ _ _ _     ≠a_____
5_ _ _ _     ≠a_____
670          ≠a_____
670          ≠a_____

No. _____
008
040          ≠a_____          ≠c_____
1_ _ _ _     ≠a_____
4_ _ _ _     ≠a_____
4_ _ _ _     ≠a_____
5_ _ _ _     ≠a_____
5_ _ _ _     ≠a_____
670          ≠a_____
670          ≠a_____

No. _____
008
040          ≠a_____          ≠c_____
1_ _ _ _     ≠a_____
4_ _ _ _     ≠a_____
4_ _ _ _     ≠a_____
5_ _ _ _     ≠a_____
5_ _ _ _     ≠a_____
670          ≠a_____
670          ≠a_____

No. _____
008
040          ≠a_____          ≠c_____
1_ _ _ _     ≠a_____
4_ _ _ _     ≠a_____
4_ _ _ _     ≠a_____
5_ _ _ _     ≠a_____
5_ _ _ _     ≠a_____
670          ≠a_____
670          ≠a_____

No. _____
008
040          ≠a_____          ≠c_____
1____          ≠a_____
4____          ≠a_____
4____          ≠a_____
5____          ≠a_____
5____          ≠a_____
670          ≠a_____
670          ≠a_____

No. _____
008
040          ≠a_____          ≠c_____
1____          ≠a_____
4____          ≠a_____
4____          ≠a_____
5____          ≠a_____
5____          ≠a_____
670          ≠a_____
670          ≠a_____

No. _____
008
040          ≠a_____          ≠c_____
1____          ≠a_____
4____          ≠a_____
4____          ≠a_____
5____          ≠a_____
5____          ≠a_____
670          ≠a_____
670          ≠a_____

No. _____
008
040          ≠a_____          ≠c_____
1____          ≠a_____
4____          ≠a_____
4____          ≠a_____
5____          ≠a_____
5____          ≠a_____
670          ≠a_____
670          ≠a_____

No. _____
008
040          ≠a_____          ≠c_____
1_ _ _ _      ≠a_____
4_ _ _ _      ≠a_____
4_ _ _ _      ≠a_____
5_ _ _ _      ≠a_____
5_ _ _ _      ≠a_____
670          ≠a_____
670          ≠a_____

No. _____
008
040          ≠a_____          ≠c_____
1_ _ _ _      ≠a_____
4_ _ _ _      ≠a_____
4_ _ _ _      ≠a_____
5_ _ _ _      ≠a_____
5_ _ _ _      ≠a_____
670          ≠a_____
670          ≠a_____

No. _____
008
040          ≠a_____          ≠c_____
1_ _ _ _      ≠a_____
4_ _ _ _      ≠a_____
4_ _ _ _      ≠a_____
5_ _ _ _      ≠a_____
5_ _ _ _      ≠a_____
670          ≠a_____
670          ≠a_____

No. _____
008
040          ≠a_____          ≠c_____
1_ _ _ _      ≠a_____
4_ _ _ _      ≠a_____
4_ _ _ _      ≠a_____
5_ _ _ _      ≠a_____
5_ _ _ _      ≠a_____
670          ≠a_____
670          ≠a_____

No. _____
008
040          ≠a_____          ≠c_____
1_ _ _ _     ≠a_____
4_ _ _ _     ≠a_____
4_ _ _ _     ≠a_____
5_ _ _ _     ≠a_____
5_ _ _ _     ≠a_____
670          ≠a_____
670          ≠a_____

No. _____
008
040          ≠a_____          ≠c_____
1_ _ _ _     ≠a_____
4_ _ _ _     ≠a_____
4_ _ _ _     ≠a_____
5_ _ _ _     ≠a_____
5_ _ _ _     ≠a_____
670          ≠a_____
670          ≠a_____

No. _____
008
040          ≠a_____          ≠c_____
1_ _ _ _     ≠a_____
4_ _ _ _     ≠a_____
4_ _ _ _     ≠a_____
5_ _ _ _     ≠a_____
5_ _ _ _     ≠a_____
670          ≠a_____
670          ≠a_____

No. _____
008
040          ≠a_____          ≠c_____
1_ _ _ _     ≠a_____
4_ _ _ _     ≠a_____
4_ _ _ _     ≠a_____
5_ _ _ _     ≠a_____
5_ _ _ _     ≠a_____
670          ≠a_____
670          ≠a_____

No. _____
008
040          ≠a_____          ≠c_____
1_ _ _ _     ≠a_____
4_ _ _ _     ≠a_____
4_ _ _ _     ≠a_____
5_ _ _ _     ≠a_____
5_ _ _ _     ≠a_____
670          ≠a_____
670          ≠a_____

No. _____
008
040          ≠a_____          ≠c_____
1_ _ _ _     ≠a_____
4_ _ _ _     ≠a_____
4_ _ _ _     ≠a_____
5_ _ _ _     ≠a_____
5_ _ _ _     ≠a_____
670          ≠a_____
670          ≠a_____

No. _____
008
040          ≠a_____          ≠c_____
1_ _ _ _     ≠a_____
4_ _ _ _     ≠a_____
4_ _ _ _     ≠a_____
5_ _ _ _     ≠a_____
5_ _ _ _     ≠a_____
670          ≠a_____
670          ≠a_____

No. _____
008
040          ≠a_____          ≠c_____
1_ _ _ _     ≠a_____
4_ _ _ _     ≠a_____
4_ _ _ _     ≠a_____
5_ _ _ _     ≠a_____
5_ _ _ _     ≠a_____
670          ≠a_____
670          ≠a_____

No. _____
008
040       ≠a_____      ≠c_____
1_ _ _ _    ≠a_____
4_ _ _ _    ≠a_____
4_ _ _ _    ≠a_____
5_ _ _ _    ≠a_____
5_ _ _ _    ≠a_____
670       ≠a_____
670       ≠a_____

No. _____
008
040       ≠a_____      ≠c_____
1_ _ _ _    ≠a_____
4_ _ _ _    ≠a_____
4_ _ _ _    ≠a_____
5_ _ _ _    ≠a_____
5_ _ _ _    ≠a_____
670       ≠a_____
670       ≠a_____

No. _____
008
040       ≠a_____      ≠c_____
1_ _ _ _    ≠a_____
4_ _ _ _    ≠a_____
4_ _ _ _    ≠a_____
5_ _ _ _    ≠a_____
5_ _ _ _    ≠a_____
670       ≠a_____
670       ≠a_____

No. _____
008
040       ≠a_____      ≠c_____
1_ _ _ _    ≠a_____
4_ _ _ _    ≠a_____
4_ _ _ _    ≠a_____
5_ _ _ _    ≠a_____
5_ _ _ _    ≠a_____
670       ≠a_____
670       ≠a_____

No. _____
008
040         ≠a_____         ≠c_____
1_ _ _ _     ≠a_____
4_ _ _ _     ≠a_____
4_ _ _ _     ≠a_____
5_ _ _ _     ≠a_____
5_ _ _ _     ≠a_____
670         ≠a_____
670         ≠a_____

No. _____
008
040         ≠a_____         ≠c_____
1_ _ _ _     ≠a_____
4_ _ _ _     ≠a_____
4_ _ _ _     ≠a_____
5_ _ _ _     ≠a_____
5_ _ _ _     ≠a_____
670         ≠a_____
670         ≠a_____

No. _____
008
040         ≠a_____         ≠c_____
1_ _ _ _     ≠a_____
4_ _ _ _     ≠a_____
4_ _ _ _     ≠a_____
5_ _ _ _     ≠a_____
5_ _ _ _     ≠a_____
670         ≠a_____
670         ≠a_____

No. _____
008
040         ≠a_____         ≠c_____
1_ _ _ _     ≠a_____
4_ _ _ _     ≠a_____
4_ _ _ _     ≠a_____
5_ _ _ _     ≠a_____
5_ _ _ _     ≠a_____
670         ≠a_____
670         ≠a_____

No. _____
008
040        ≠a_____        ≠c_____
1_ _ _ _        ≠a_____
4_ _ _ _        ≠a_____
4_ _ _ _        ≠a_____
5_ _ _ _        ≠a_____
5_ _ _ _        ≠a_____
670        ≠a_____
670        ≠a_____

No. _____
008
040        ≠a_____        ≠c_____
1_ _ _ _        ≠a_____
4_ _ _ _        ≠a_____
4_ _ _ _        ≠a_____
5_ _ _ _        ≠a_____
5_ _ _ _        ≠a_____
670        ≠a_____
670        ≠a_____

No. _____
008
040        ≠a_____        ≠c_____
1_ _ _ _        ≠a_____
4_ _ _ _        ≠a_____
4_ _ _ _        ≠a_____
5_ _ _ _        ≠a_____
5_ _ _ _        ≠a_____
670        ≠a_____
670        ≠a_____

No. _____
008
040        ≠a_____        ≠c_____
1_ _ _ _        ≠a_____
4_ _ _ _        ≠a_____
4_ _ _ _        ≠a_____
5_ _ _ _        ≠a_____
5_ _ _ _        ≠a_____
670        ≠a_____
670        ≠a_____

No. _____
008
040        ≠a_____        ≠c_____
1____      ≠a_____
4____      ≠a_____
4____      ≠a_____
5____      ≠a_____
5____      ≠a_____
670        ≠a_____
670        ≠a_____

No. _____
008
040        ≠a_____        ≠c_____
1____      ≠a_____
4____      ≠a_____
4____      ≠a_____
5____      ≠a_____
5____      ≠a_____
670        ≠a_____
670        ≠a_____

No. _____
008
040        ≠a_____        ≠c_____
1____      ≠a_____
4____      ≠a_____
4____      ≠a_____
5____      ≠a_____
5____      ≠a_____
670        ≠a_____
670        ≠a_____

No. _____
008
040        ≠a_____        ≠c_____
1____      ≠a_____
4____      ≠a_____
4____      ≠a_____
5____      ≠a_____
5____      ≠a_____
670        ≠a_____
670        ≠a_____

No. _____
008
040        ≠a_____        ≠c_____
1_ _ _ _        ≠a_____
4_ _ _ _        ≠a_____
4_ _ _ _        ≠a_____
5_ _ _ _        ≠a_____
5_ _ _ _        ≠a_____
670        ≠a_____
670        ≠a_____

No. _____
008
040        ≠a_____        ≠c_____
1_ _ _ _        ≠a_____
4_ _ _ _        ≠a_____
4_ _ _ _        ≠a_____
5_ _ _ _        ≠a_____
5_ _ _ _        ≠a_____
670        ≠a_____
670        ≠a_____

No. _____
008
040        ≠a_____        ≠c_____
1_ _ _ _        ≠a_____
4_ _ _ _        ≠a_____
4_ _ _ _        ≠a_____
5_ _ _ _        ≠a_____
5_ _ _ _        ≠a_____
670        ≠a_____
670        ≠a_____

No. _____
008
040        ≠a_____        ≠c_____
1_ _ _ _        ≠a_____
4_ _ _ _        ≠a_____
4_ _ _ _        ≠a_____
5_ _ _ _        ≠a_____
5_ _ _ _        ≠a_____
670        ≠a_____
670        ≠a_____

No. _____
008
040          ≠a_____          ≠c_____
1_ _ _ _     ≠a_____
4_ _ _ _     ≠a_____
4_ _ _ _     ≠a_____
5_ _ _ _     ≠a_____
5_ _ _ _     ≠a_____
670          ≠a_____
670          ≠a_____

No. _____
008
040          ≠a_____          ≠c_____
1_ _ _ _     ≠a_____
4_ _ _ _     ≠a_____
4_ _ _ _     ≠a_____
5_ _ _ _     ≠a_____
5_ _ _ _     ≠a_____
670          ≠a_____
670          ≠a_____

No. _____
008
040          ≠a_____          ≠c_____
1_ _ _ _     ≠a_____
4_ _ _ _     ≠a_____
4_ _ _ _     ≠a_____
5_ _ _ _     ≠a_____
5_ _ _ _     ≠a_____
670          ≠a_____
670          ≠a_____

No. _____
008
040          ≠a_____          ≠c_____
1_ _ _ _     ≠a_____
4_ _ _ _     ≠a_____
4_ _ _ _     ≠a_____
5_ _ _ _     ≠a_____
5_ _ _ _     ≠a_____
670          ≠a_____
670          ≠a_____

## 126  Templates

No. _____
008
040  &ne;a_____   &ne;c_____
1_ _ _ _ &ne;a_____
4_ _ _ _ &ne;a_____
4_ _ _ _ &ne;a_____
5_ _ _ _ &ne;a_____
5_ _ _ _ &ne;a_____
670  &ne;a_____
670  &ne;a_____

No. _____
008
040  &ne;a_____   &ne;c_____
1_ _ _ _ &ne;a_____
4_ _ _ _ &ne;a_____
4_ _ _ _ &ne;a_____
5_ _ _ _ &ne;a_____
5_ _ _ _ &ne;a_____
670  &ne;a_____
670  &ne;a_____

No. _____
008
040  &ne;a_____   &ne;c_____
1_ _ _ _ &ne;a_____
4_ _ _ _ &ne;a_____
4_ _ _ _ &ne;a_____
5_ _ _ _ &ne;a_____
5_ _ _ _ &ne;a_____
670  &ne;a_____
670  &ne;a_____

No. _____
008
040  &ne;a_____   &ne;c_____
1_ _ _ _ &ne;a_____
4_ _ _ _ &ne;a_____
4_ _ _ _ &ne;a_____
5_ _ _ _ &ne;a_____
5_ _ _ _ &ne;a_____
670  &ne;a_____
670  &ne;a_____

No. _____
008
040        ≠a_____      ≠c_____
1\_ \_ \_ \_    ≠a_____
4\_ \_ \_ \_    ≠a_____
4\_ \_ \_ \_    ≠a_____
5\_ \_ \_ \_    ≠a_____
5\_ \_ \_ \_    ≠a_____
670        ≠a_____
670        ≠a_____

No. _____
008
040        ≠a_____      ≠c_____
1\_ \_ \_ \_    ≠a_____
4\_ \_ \_ \_    ≠a_____
4\_ \_ \_ \_    ≠a_____
5\_ \_ \_ \_    ≠a_____
5\_ \_ \_ \_    ≠a_____
670        ≠a_____
670        ≠a_____

No. _____
008
040        ≠a_____      ≠c_____
1\_ \_ \_ \_    ≠a_____
4\_ \_ \_ \_    ≠a_____
4\_ \_ \_ \_    ≠a_____
5\_ \_ \_ \_    ≠a_____
5\_ \_ \_ \_    ≠a_____
670        ≠a_____
670        ≠a_____

No. _____
008
040        ≠a_____      ≠c_____
1\_ \_ \_ \_    ≠a_____
4\_ \_ \_ \_    ≠a_____
4\_ \_ \_ \_    ≠a_____
5\_ \_ \_ \_    ≠a_____
5\_ \_ \_ \_    ≠a_____
670        ≠a_____
670        ≠a_____

No. _____
008
040          ≠a_____          ≠c_____
1_ _ _ _          ≠a_____
4_ _ _ _          ≠a_____
4_ _ _ _          ≠a_____
5_ _ _ _          ≠a_____
5_ _ _ _          ≠a_____
670          ≠a_____
670          ≠a_____

No. _____
008
040          ≠a_____          ≠c_____
1_ _ _ _          ≠a_____
4_ _ _ _          ≠a_____
4_ _ _ _          ≠a_____
5_ _ _ _          ≠a_____
5_ _ _ _          ≠a_____
670          ≠a_____
670          ≠a_____

No. _____
008
040          ≠a_____          ≠c_____
1_ _ _ _          ≠a_____
4_ _ _ _          ≠a_____
4_ _ _ _          ≠a_____
5_ _ _ _          ≠a_____
5_ _ _ _          ≠a_____
670          ≠a_____
670          ≠a_____

No. _____
008
040          ≠a_____          ≠c_____
1_ _ _ _          ≠a_____
4_ _ _ _          ≠a_____
4_ _ _ _          ≠a_____
5_ _ _ _          ≠a_____
5_ _ _ _          ≠a_____
670          ≠a_____
670          ≠a_____

# BIBLIOGRAPHY

99% of being thought a genius consists
of knowing who to ask!"
> —Trey Lewis, Director,
> Red River Parish Library

## General Materials

Byrne, Deborah J. *MARC Manual: Understanding and Using MARC Records.* 2nd ed. Englewood, CO: Libraries Unlimited, 1998.

Evans, G. Edward, Sheila S. Inter, and Jean Weihs. *Introduction to Technical Services.* 7th ed. Englewood, CO: Libraries Unlimited, 2002.

Fritz, Deborah A. *Cataloging with AACR2R and USMARC: For Books, Computer Files, Serials, Sound Recordings, Video Recordings.* Chicago: American Library Association, 1998.

Fritz, Deborah A., and Richard J. Fritz. *MARC 21 for Everyone: A Practical Guide.* Chicago: American Library Association, 2003.

Furrier, Betty. *Understanding MARC Bibliographic: Machine Readable Cataloging.* 6th ed. Washington, DC: Library of Congress, 2000.

Gilded, Matthew E. *MARC Content Designation.* 2nd ed. Washington, DC: Library of Congress, 2002.

Harshen, Arnold, and Barbara Winters. *Outsourcing Library Technical Services: A How-to-Do-It Manual for Librarians.* New York: Neal-Schuman, 1996.

Hunter, Gregory S. *Developing and Maintaining Practical Archives: A How-to-Do-It Manual.* 2nd ed. New York: Neal-Schuman, 2003.

Intner, Sheila, and Jean Weihs. *Special Libraries: A Cataloging Guide.* Englewood, CO: Libraries Unlimited, 1998.

McRae, Linda, and Lynda S. White, eds. *ArtMARC Sourcebook: Cataloging Art, Architecture and Their Visual Images.* Chicago: American Library Association, 1998.

Millsap, Larry, and Terry Ellen Ferl. *Descriptive Cataloging for the AACR2R and the Integrated Marc Format: A How-to-Do-It Workbook.* Rev. ed. New York: Neal-Schuman, 1997.

Piepenburg, Scott. *Easy MARC: Incorporating Format Integration.* 3rd ed. San Jose, CA: F&W Associates, 1999.

Schultz, Lois, and Sarah Shaw, comps. *Cataloging Sheet Music: Guidelines for Use with AACR2 and the MARC Format.* Lanham, MD: Scarecrow Press; [United States]: Music Library Association, 2003.

Stein, Barbara L., and Risa W. Brown. *Running a School Library Media Center: A How-to-Do-It Manual.* 2nd ed. New York: Neal-Schuman, 2002.

Stielow, Frederick. *Building Digital Archives, Descriptions, & Displays: A How-to-Do-It Manual for Archivists & Librarians.* New York: Neal-Schuman, 2003.

Weber, Mary Beth. *Cataloging Nonprint and Internet Resources: A How-to-Do-It Manual for Librarians.* New York: Neal-Schuman, 2002.

Weitz, Jay. *Music Coding and Tagging: MARC 21 Content Designation for Scores and Sound Recordings.* 2nd ed. Belle Plaine, MN: Soldier Creek Press, 2001.

## Periodicals and Serials

*Cataloging & Classification Quarterly.* Binghamton, NY: Haworth Press, 1980– . Quarterly.

*Cataloging Service Bulletin.* Washington, DC: Library of Congress, 1978– . Quarterly.

*Library Resources & Technical Services.* Chicago: American Library Association, 1982– . Quarterly.

*Technical Services Quarterly.* Binghamton, NY: Haworth Press, 1983– . Quarterly.

*Technicalities.* Kansas City, MO: Media Services Publications, 1981– . Monthly.

# ANSWER KEY
# DESCRIPTIVE CATALOGING

## 1.1. Families of Tags Exercise—Answers

| | |
|---|---|
| 1.1.1. | 6xx |
| 1.1.2. | 260 |
| 1.1.3. | 4xx |
| 1.1.4. | 9xx |
| 1.1.5. | 1xx |
| 1.1.6. | 0xx |
| 1.1.7. | 8xx |
| 1.1.8. | 3xx |
| 1.1.9. | 7xx |
| 1.1.10. | 24x |
| 1.1.11. | 25x |
| 1.1.12. | 5xx |
| 1.1.13. | Locally defined fields |
| 1.1.14. | Computer utilization fields |
| 1.1.15. | Added entry fields |
| 1.1.16. | Title fields |
| 1.1.17. | Notes fields |
| 1.1.18. | Main entry fields |
| 1.1.19. | Series added entry fields |
| 1.1.20. | Edition and scale fields |
| 1.1.21. | Physical description fields |
| 1.1.22. | Subject heading fields |
| 1.1.23. | Series fields |
| 1.1.24. | Imprint field |
| 1.1.25. | Uniform title entry |
| 1.1.26. | Personal name |
| 1.1.27. | Conference or meeting name |

| 1.1.28. | Corporate name |
|---------|----------------|
| 1.1.29. | x30 |
| 1.1.30. | x10 |
| 1.1.31. | x11 |
| 1.1.32. | x00 |

# 1.2.   008 Field, Bibliographic Records, Exercise Set 1 Answers

| 1.2.1. | a. | 440629 |
|--------|----|--------|
|        | b. | 860501 |
|        | c. | 641111 |
|        | d. | 700527 |
|        | e. | 960923 |
|        | f. | 780308 |

| 1.2.2. | a. | r | 1997 | 1991 |
|--------|----|---|------|------|
|        | b. | m | 1981 | 1987 |
|        | c. | s | 1997 |      |
|        | d. | c | 1963 | 9999 |
|        | e. | q | 1970 | 1979 |
|        | f. | q | 1900 | 1950 |
|        | g. | p | 1973 | 1986 |
|        | h. | n | [blank] | [blank] |

| 1.2.3. | a. | mou |
|--------|----|-----|
|        | b. | nju |
|        | c. | aru |
|        | d. | mdu |
|        | e. | mau |
|        | f. | flu |
|        | g. | enk |
|        | h. | fr |
|        | i. | ch |
|        | j. | vi |
|        | k. | bn |

1.2.4.  a.    bfj
        b.    cdeg
        c.    a
        d.    hijk
        e.    aekl
        f.    agm
        g.    bde
        h.    acfh
        i.    cjp
        j.    bdg

1.2.5.  a.    j
        b.    b
        c.    d
        d.    e
        e.    f
        f.    a
        g.    d
        h.    g
        i.    c
        j.    b

1.2.6.  a.    b
        b.    f
        c.    a
        d.    d
        e.    c
        f.    s

1.2.7.  a.    i
        b.    k
        c.    f
        d.    c
        e.    s
        f.    e
        g.    l
        h.    v
        i.    j
        j.    b

1.2.8.    a.    l
          b.    f
          c.    s
          d.    i
          e.    ____
          f.    c
          g.    m

1.2.9.    a.    a
          b.    c
          c.    c
          d.    b
          e.    d
          f.    ____

1.2.10.   a.    fre
          b.    vie
          c.    eng
          d.    chi
          e.    spa
          f.    ger
          g.    ita
          h.    ara

1.2.11.   a.    s
          b.    d
          c.    x
          d.    o
          e.    ____

1.2.12.   a.    d
          b.    ____
          c.    c
          d.    d

1.2.13.   a.    G    Type of date/Publication status
          b.    B    Festschrift
          c.    G    Place of publication, production or execution
          d.    B    Conference publication

| e. | G | Date entered on file |
|----|---|---------------------|
| f. | G | Language |
| g. | B | Illustrations |
| h. | G | Cataloging source |
| i. | B | Nature of contents |
| j. | G | Date 1 |
| k. | B | Undefined |
| l. | G | Modified record |
| m. | G | Date 2 |
| n. | B | Index |
| o. | B | Government publication |
| p. | B | Target audience |
| q. | B | Biography |
| r. | B | Form of item |
| s. | B | Literary form |

# 008 Field, Bibliographic Records, Exercise Set 2 Answers

| 1.2.14. | 008 | . . . . . . s1996 . . . . nyua . . . . . b . . . . 001 . 0 . eng . d |
|---------|-----|----|
| 1.2.15. | 008 | . . . . . . s1997 . . . .nyu . . . . . . . . 000 . 0 . eng . d |
| 1.2.16. | 008 | . . . . . . s1994 . . . .msuab . . . b . . . . 001 . 0 . eng . d |
| 1.2.17. | 008 | . . . . . . s1995 . . . .nyub . . . . . . . . 001 . 0 . eng . d |
| 1.2.18. | 008 | . . . . . . s1996 . . . .ohuacf . . . b . . . 000 . 0 . eng . d |
| 1.2.19. | 008 | . . . . . . s1997 . . . . fr . ab . . . . b . . . . 001 . 0 . fre . d |
| 1.2.20. | 008 | . . . . . . s1993 . . . .utuab . . . . . . . 001 . 0 . eng . d |
| 1.2.21. | 008 | . . . . . . s1997 . . . .ilu . . . . . b . . . . 001 . 0 . eng . d |
| 1.2.22. | 008 | . . . . . . s1997 . . . .enkaf . . . . b . . . . 001 . 0 . eng . d |
| 1.2.23. | 008 | . . . . . . s1997 . . . .dcu . . . . . . . . . f 000 . 0 . eng . d |
| 1.2.24. | 008 | . . . . . . s1996 . . . .moua . . . . . . . . 001 . 0 . eng . d |
| 1.2.25. | 008 | . . . . . . s1997 . . . .akuaf . . . . . . . 000 . 0 . eng . d |

# 1.4. Tagging Exercise Answers

## Main Entries

| | | |
|---|---|---|
| 1.4.1 | 100 1 | ≠a Dow, Elizabeth. |
| 1.4.2 | 100 1 | ≠a Vargas Llosa, Mario. |
| 1.4.3. | 110 1 | ≠a Nebraska ≠b Legislature. ≠b Senate. |
| 1.4.4. | 110 2 | ≠a Nebraska  Academy of Sciences. |
| 1.4.5. | 110 2 | ≠a Kisatchie National Forest. |
| 1.4.6. | 100 1 | ≠a Magnus, Olaus, ≠ d 1490-1557. |
| 1.4.7. | 100 1 | ≠a Spate, Gaspar J. ≠q (Gaspar Julius), ≠d 1881-1956. |
| 1.4.8. | 100 0 | ≠a Paul, ≠c of Byzantium. |
| 1.4.9. | 110 2 | ≠a Who (Musical group) |
| 1.4.10. | 110 1 | ≠a Shreveport (La.). ≠b Police Jury. ≠b Library Committee. |
| 1.4.11. | 110 2 | ≠a Regional Planning Council for Southwest Louisiana. |
| 1.4.12. | 130 0 | ≠a Bible. ≠p O.T. ≠p Exodus. |
| 1.4.13. | 100 1 | ≠a Pennyfeather, John, ≠c Sir, ≠d 1770-1820. |
| 1.4.14. | 111 2 | ≠a Monroe Bowling Tournament ≠d (1983 : ≠c Monroe, La.) |

## Title Statements

| | | |
|---|---|---|
| 1.4.15. | 245 10 | ≠a Guide to writing tree ordinances / ≠c prepared by Buck Abbey. |
| 1.4.16. | 245 10 | ≠a "Blood will tell!" / ≠c Joseph Bosco. |
| 1.4.17. | 245 00 | ≠a Reflections in time / ≠c Elizabeth Crane, editor. |
| 1.4.18. | 245 14 | ≠a The vampire companion / ≠c Katherine Ramsland. |
| 1.4.19. | 245 15 | ≠a The "Gimme something mister" guide to Mardi Gras / ≠c by Arthur Hardy. |
| 1.4.20. | 245 10 | ≠a Tell me more ; or, The Hollywood gossip book / ≠c by Nancy Davis Reagan. |
| 1.4.21. | 245 14 | ≠a The stumpin' grounds : ≠b a memoir of New Orleans' Ninth Ward / ≠ c by Russell E. Wyman. |
| 1.4.22. | 245 10 | ≠a ... So I told him no : ≠ b the trail to the Vice-Presidency / ≠c by Al Gore. |
| 1.4.23. | 245 10 | ≠a Fort Claiborne / ≠c prepared by Cecil Atkinson. *[If you think of Atkinson as an editor, code it 00.]* |
| 1.4.24. | 245 00 | ≠a Hobnails and helmets / ≠c William H. Burkhart ... [et al.]. |
| 1.4.25. | 245 14 | ≠a The analysis of the law : ≠b penalties for transgressors / ≠c Sir Matthew Hale. |

## Publication, Distribution, Etc.

| | | |
|---|---|---|
| 1.4.26. | 260 | ≠a New York : ≠b Greenwillow Press, ≠c [1949]. |
| 1.4.27. | 260 | ≠a Washington D.C. : ≠b U.S. Dept. of Agriculture : [for sale by the U.S. G.P.O.], ≠c 1964. |
| 1.4.28. | 260 | ≠a London : ≠ b Haynes ; ≠a Brookstone, Conn. : ≠b Auto Museum, ≠c c1997. |
| 1.4.29. | 260 | ≠a [Bohemia, La.?] : ≠b L.B. Oppenheimer, ≠c 1957. |
| 1.4.30. | 260 | ≠a [Albuquerque] : ≠b University of New Mexico Press, ≠c 1985. |
| 1.4.31. | 260 | ≠a Toronto ; New York : ≠b Bantam, ≠c c1952. |
| 1.4.32. | 260 | ≠a [S.l. : ≠b s.n.], ≠c 1935. |
| 1.4.33. | 260 | ≠a Paris : ≠b LeBlanc et cie., ≠c 1935, c1899. |
| 1.4.34. | 260 | ≠a Bayou Manchac, La. : ≠b [s.n., ≠c 19—?] |
| 1.4.35. | 260 | ≠a Alexandria, La. : ≠b Alexandria Museum of Art, ≠c c1977. |

## Physical Description

| | | |
|---|---|---|
| 1.4.36. | 300 | ≠a 3 v. ; ≠c 30 cm. + ≠e atlas (301 leaves of plates : maps) |
| 1.4.37. | 300 | ≠a 64 p. : ≠b maps ; ≠c 32 cm. |
| 1.4.38. | 300 | ≠a 65 leaves, 102 p., [8] p. of plates : ≠b ill. ; ≠c 16 cm. |
| 1.4.39. | 300 | ≠a xlv, 789 p. : ≠b ill., ports., maps (1 fold.) ; ≠c 13 cm. |
| 1.4.40. | 300 | ≠a 251 p. ; ≠c 22 cm. |
| 1.4.41. | 300 | ≠a 1 videocassette (22 min.) : ≠b sd., col. ; ≠c ½ in. |
| 1.4.42. | 300 | ≠a 1 microscope slide : ≠b glass ; ≠c 8 x 3 cm. |
| 1.4.43. | 300 | ≠a 1 game (15 pieces) : ≠ b col., cardboard ; ≠c 9 x 12 in. |
| 1.4.44. | 300 | ≠a v. : ≠b ill., maps ; ≠c 28 cm. |
| 1.4.45. | 300 | ≠a 2 film reels (60 min. ea.) : ≠ b sd., b&w ; ≠c 16 mm. |
| 1.4.46. | 300 | ≠a ii, 14, vi, 61 p. : ≠ b ill., facsims. ; ≠c 12 x 16 cm. |
| 1.4.47. | 300 | ≠a 1 score : ≠b 16 p. of music ; ≠c 28 cm. + ≠e 1 sound disk. |
| 1.4.48. | 300 | ≠a 1 v. (various pagings) ; ≠c 26 cm. |
| 1.4.49. | 300 | ≠a 1 sound disc (65 min.) : ≠b digital, stereo. ; ≠c 4 3/4 in. |

## Notes

| | | |
|---|---|---|
| 1.4.50. | 500 | ≠a Title from disk label. |
| 1.4.51. | 520 | ≠a Summary: Biography of Shaquille O'Neal. |
| 1.4.52. | 501 | ≠a With: Only in your arms / Lisa Kleypas. |
| 1.4.53. | 504 | ≠a Includes discography (p. 547-569). |
| 1.4.54. | 500 | ≠a Title supplied by cataloger. |

| 1.4.55. | 500 | ≠a Reprint. Originally published: Boston : Grey, 1896. |
| 1.4.56. | 511 | ≠a Cast: Ronald Reagan, Bill Clinton, George W. Bush. |
| 1.4.57. | 505 0 | ≠a Contents: Hey look me over -- Louisiana hayride -- Cajun two-step -- When the saints go marching in -- Bayou blues -- LSU Alma Mater. |
| 1.4.58. | 502 | ≠a Ph.D. (Library Science)—Duke University, 1978. |
| 1.4.59. | 500 | ≠a Includes index. |
| 1.4.60. | 500 | ≠a Editor, 1987- : Bobby Ferguson. |
| 1.4.61. | 505 10 | ≠t Introduction -- ≠t Questioning Kubrick's clockwork / ≠c S.Y. McDougal -- ≠t Clockwork … ticking / ≠c R. Kolker -- ≠t Cultural productions / ≠c J. Staiger -- ≠t Erotics of violence / ≠c M. DeRosia -- ≠t Art cinema / ≠c K. Gabbard |

## Subject Descriptors

| 1.4.62. | 600 1 0 | ≠a Lincoln, Abraham, ≠d 1809-1865. |
| 1.4.63. | 650  0 | ≠a Gardening ≠z Louisiana ≠z New Orleans. |
| 1.4.64. | 610 1 0 | ≠a Louisiana. ≠b Office of the Lieutenant Governor. |
| 1.4.65. | 650  0 | ≠a Cookery (Oysters) |
| 1.4.66. | 610 2 0 | ≠a Daughters of the Confederacy. ≠ b Louisiana Chapter. ≠b Baton Rouge Post. |
| 1.4.67. | 651  0 | ≠a Port Allen (La.) ≠x Politics and government. |
| 1.4.68. | 651  0 | ≠a Alexandria (La.) ≠x History ≠y Civil War, 1861-1865. |
| 1.4.69. | 600 1 0 | ≠a Lawrence, Elizabeth, ≠d 1904-1985. |
| 1.4.70. | 650  0 | ≠a Physically handicapped artists ≠z Louisiana. |
| 1.4.71. | 600 3 0 | ≠a Burford family. |
| 1.4.72. | 651  0 | ≠a Lafourche Parish (La.) ≠x Description and travel. |
| 1.4.73. | 610 1 0 | ≠a Lafayette Parish (La.). ≠b Office of the Mayor. |
| 1.4.74. | 610 2 0 | ≠a New Tickfaw Baptist Church (Livingston Parish, La.) |
| 1.4.75. | 600 0 0 | ≠a Joan, ≠c of Arc, Saint. |
| 1.4.76. | 651  0 | ≠a Pilottown (La.) ≠x History. |
| 1.4.77. | 600 1 0 | ≠a Hunter, Bruce, ≠d 1958- |
| 1.4.78. | 651  0 | ≠a East Feliciana Parish (La.) ≠x Economic aspects. |
| 1.4.79. | 650  0 | ≠a Hurricanes ≠z Louisiana ≠z Cheniere Caminada. |
| 1.4.80. | 611 2 0 | ≠a Grand Isle Tarpon Rodeo ≠n (26th : ≠ d 1979) |
| 1.4.81. | 630 0 0 | ≠a Bible. ≠p O.T. ≠p Genesis. |

## Full Records

**1.4.82.**

| | |
|---|---|
| 110 1 | ≠a Alabama. ≠b Alcoholic Beverage Control Board. |
| 245 1 0 | ≠a Annual beer report / ≠c Alabama Alcoholic Beverage Control Board. |
| 260 | ≠a Montgomery, Ala. : ≠b The Board. |
| 300 | ≠a v. ; ≠c 28 cm. |
| 310 | ≠a Annual |
| 500 | ≠a Description based on: October 1, 1977-Sept. 30, 1978. |
| 500 | ≠a Title from cover. |
| 500 | ≠a Report year ends Sept. 30. |
| 650 0 | ≠a Brewing industry ≠z Alabama ≠v Statistics. |

**1.4.83.**

| | |
|---|---|
| 245 0 0 | ≠a Marching bands & corps. |
| 246 1 0 | ≠a Marching bands and corps. |
| 260 | ≠a [Jacksonville, Fla. : ≠b River City Publications], ≠c 1967- |
| 300 | ≠a v. : ≠b ill. ; ≠c 28 cm. |
| 310 | ≠a Monthly. |
| 362 0 | ≠a 1967- |
| 500 | ≠a Includes index. |
| 650 0 | ≠a Bands (Music) |

**1.4.84.**

| | |
|---|---|
| 100 1 | ≠a Milne, A. A. ≠q (Alan Alexander), ≠d 1882-1956. |
| 245 1 4 | ≠a The house at Pooh Corner / ≠c by A.A. Milne ; illustrated by Kate Greenaway. |
| 260 | ≠a Chicago, Ill. : ≠b Children's Press, ≠c c1983. |
| 300 | ≠a 128 p. : ≠b ill. ; ≠c 21 cm. |
| 440 _ 0 | ≠a World's greatest classics |
| 700 1 | ≠a Greenaway, Kate. |

**1.4.85.**

| | |
|---|---|
| 100 1 | ≠a Grahame, Kenneth. |
| 245 1 4 | ≠a The wind in the willows / ≠c by Kenneth Grahame ; illustrated by Robert J. Lee. |
| 260 | ≠a New York : ≠b Dell, ≠c 1973, c1969. |

| 300 | ≠a 244 p. : ≠ b ill. ; ≠c 19 cm. |
|---|---|
| 500 | ≠a "A Yearling book." |

**1.4.86.**

| 100 1 | ≠a Alford, Gilbert K. |
|---|---|
| 245 1 0 | ≠a Alford ancestors and descendants : ≠b Jacob and Alvina Alford, the Allfords, and related families / ≠c by Gil and Anna Alford. |
| 250 | ≠a Rev. ed., with corrections. |
| 260 | ≠a [S.l.] : ≠b G.K. Alford, ≠c [1986?] |
| 300 | ≠a x, 279 p. : ≠b ports., facsims., geneal. tables ; ≠c 28 cm. |
| 500 | ≠a Includes indexes. |
| 600 3 0 | ≠a Alford family. |
| 651  0 | ≠a Red River Parish (La.) ≠v Genealogy. |
| 650  0 | ≠a Marriage records ≠z Louisiana ≠z Red River Parish. |
| 700 1 | ≠a Alford, Anna. |

**1.4.87.**

| 100 1 | ≠a Stratton, Joanna L. |
|---|---|
| 245 1 0 | ≠a Pioneer women : ≠b voices from the Kansas frontier / ≠c Joanna L. Stratton ; introduced by Arthur M. Schlesinger, Jr. |
| 250 | ≠a 1st ed. |
| 260 | ≠a New York : ≠b Simon & Schuster, ≠c c1981. |
| 300 | ≠a 319 p., [16] leaves of plates : ≠b ill. ; ≠c 24 cm. |
| 504 | ≠a Includes bibliographical references (p. [305]-307) and index. |
| 650  0 | ≠a Women ≠z Kansas ≠x History. |
| 650  0 | ≠a Pioneers ≠z Kansas ≠x History. |

**1.4.88.**

| 245 0 4 | ≠a The Bishop's bounty / ≠c compiled by The Bishop's Bounty Cookbook Committee, Saint Mary's Parents' Group, Inc., Saint Mary's Training School for Retarded Children. |
|---|---|
| 260 | ≠a Alexandria, La. : ≠b Saint Mary's Parents' Group, ≠c c1987. |
| 300 | ≠a 318 p. : ≠b ill. ; ≠c 24 cm. |
| 500 | ≠a Includes index. |
| 650  0 | ≠a Cookery, American ≠x Louisiana style. |
| 710 2 | ≠a Saint Mary's Training School for Retarded Children (Alexandria, La.). ≠b Saint Mary's Parents' Group. |

**1.4.89.**

| | |
|---|---|
| 245 0 4 | ≠a Les blues de Balfa  ≠h [videorecording] :  ≠b with Cajun visits/Visites Cajun. |
| 260 | ≠a San Francisco, Calif. :  ≠b Aginsky Productions,  ≠c c1983, c1981. |
| 300 | ≠a 1 videocassette (20, 16 min.) :  ≠b sd., col. ;  ≠c ½ in. |
| 538 | ≠a VHS format. |
| 520 | ≠a Summary: The story of the Balfa Brothers, and a visit to Cajun country. |
| 650   0 | ≠a Cajuns  ≠z Louisiana. |
| 600 1 0 | ≠a Balfa, Dewey. |
| 610 2 0 | ≠a Balfa Brothers (Musical group) |
| 740 0 2 | ≠a Cajun visits. |
| 740 0 2 | ≠a Visites Cajun. |

**1.4.90.**

| | |
|---|---|
| 100 1 | ≠a Darensbourg, Joe,  ≠d 1906-1985. |
| 245 1 0 | ≠a Jazz odyssey :  ≠b the autobiography of Joe Darensbourg / ≠ c as told to Peter Vacher. |
| 246 1 0 | ≠a Telling it like it is |
| 260 | ≠a Baton Rouge : ≠ b Louisiana State University Press,  ≠c 1988, c1987. |
| 300 | ≠a vi, 231 p., [32] p. of plates :  ≠b ports. ;  ≠c 25 cm. |
| 504 | ≠a Includes bibliographical references (p. [197]-207) and index. |
| 500 | ≠a Published in England under the title: Telling it like it is. |
| 600 1 0 | ≠a Darensbourg, Joe, ≠ d 1906-1985. |
| 650   0 | ≠a Jazz musicians  ≠z Louisiana  ≠z New Orleans. |
| 700 1 | ≠a Vacher, Peter,  ≠d 1937- |

**1.4.91.**

| | |
|---|---|
| 100 1 | ≠a Kilbourne, Richard Holcomb. |
| 245 1 2 | ≠a A history of the Louisiana Civil Code :  ≠b the formative years, 1803-1839 /  ≠c Richard Holcomb Kilbourne, Jr. |
| 260 | ≠a [Baton Rouge] :  ≠b Publications Institute, Paul M. Hebert Law Center, Louisiana State University,  ≠c c1987. |
| 300 | ≠a xv, 268 p. ;  ≠c 24 cm. |
| 500 | ≠a "Prepared under the auspices of the Center of Civil Law Studies." -- t.p. |
| 504 | ≠a Includes bibliographical references and index. |
| 650   0 | ≠a Civil law  ≠z Louisiana  ≠x History. |
| 650   0 | ≠a Civil law  ≠z Louisiana  ≠x Codification  x History. |
| 710 2 | ≠a Paul M. Hebert Law Center. |

# 1.5.   Series Exercise Answers

| 1.5.1 | 490 0_ | ≠a Rechtschistorisch Instituut ; ≠v serie 1 |
|---|---|---|
| 1.5.2. | 440 _0 | ≠a SUNY series in new directions in crime and justice studies |
| 1.5.3. | 800 1_ | ≠a Bentham, Jeremy, ≠d 1748-1832. ≠t Defense of usury |
| | 440 _0 | ≠a Defense of usury |
| 1.5.4. | 440 _0 | ≠a AAR studies in religion / American Academy of Religion |
| | 810 2_ | ≠a American Academy of Religion. ≠t AAR studies in religion |
| 1.5.5. | 440 _0 | ≠a Inspector Henry Tibbett mystery |
| 1.5.6. | 400 10 | ≠a Lane, Roger. ≠t History of crime and criminal justice series |
| 1.5.7. | 440 _0 | ≠a Prehistoric animals ; ≠v vol. 3 |
| 1.5.8. | 490 1_ | ≠a Medical problems. pt. 2, Blood problems / Suellen Probity |
| | 800 1_ | ≠a Probity, Suellen. ≠t Medical problems. ≠n pt. 2, ≠p Blood problems |
| 1.5.9. | 490 0_ | ≠a Contemporary questions / J. Wesley Smith |
| 1.5.10. | 490 1_ | ≠a VGM career books (VGM Career Horizons) |
| | 830 1_ | ≠a VGM career books |
| 1.5.11. | 440 _0 | ≠a Smithsonian guides |
| 1.5.12. | 490 1_ | ≠a A Macmillan reference book |
| | 830 _0 | ≠a Macmillan reference books |
| 1.5.13. | 490 0_ | ≠a Betterway woodworking plans series |
| | 490 1_ | ≠a Woodworking plans series |
| | 830 _0 | ≠a Betterway woodworking plans series |
| 1.5.14. | 440 _0 | ≠a Smithsonian guide to historic America ; ≠v vol. 1 |
| 1.5.15. | 490 1_ | ≠a Civil service test tutor (Arco Publishing House) |
| | 830 _0 | ≠a Civil service test tutor |
| 1.5.16. | 440 _0 | ≠a Chilton's total car care |
| | 490 0_ | ≠a Total car care |
| 1.5.17. | 440 _0 | ≠a Mitchell manuals for the automotive professional |
| 1.5.18. | 440 _0 | ≠a D.A.E. research report |
| | 490 0_ | ≠a Research report / Louisiana State Agricultural Center, Louisiana Agricultural Experiment Station, Dept. of Agricultural Economics and Agribusiness |
| 1.5.19. | 490 1_ | ≠a Information series / Louisiana State University Agricultural Center, Louisiana Agricultural Experiment Station, Department of Agricultural Economics and Agribusiness |
| | 830 _0 | ≠a A.E.A. information series |
| 1.5.20. | 490 1_ | ≠a Guitar tunes for country players / Eric Babin |
| | 800 1_ | ≠a Babin, Eric. ≠t Guitar tunes for country players |

# 1.6.   Error Identification Exercise Answers

| 1.6.1. | 100 1 | ≠a Smith, John,  ≠(z) 1956- | d |
| 1.6.2. | (110) 1 | ≠a Garcia Williams, John. | 100 |
| 1.6.3. | 110 (2) | ≠a Port Allen (La.).  ≠b Parish Council. | 1 |
| 1.6.4. | 100 (2) | ≠a Minnie Pearl, ≠d 1921-1967. | 0 |
| 1.6.5. | 111 (1) | ≠a Basketball championship  ≠d (1995) | 2 |
| 1.6.6. | (240) 12 | ≠a A dictionary of dogs. | 245 |
| 1.6.7. | 245 1(0) | ≠a The horse runs /  ≠c John Equus. | 4 |
| 1.6.8. | 245 10 | ≠(b) Everybody wins! /  ≠c Polly Tishan. | a |
| 1.6.9. | 246 1(4) | ≠a You @#$%^&*!!! | 0 |
| 1.6.10. | 245 12 | ≠a A man for all seasons /  ≠(b) Jim Doe. | c |
| 1.6.11. | 260 | ≠a New York :  ≠b( ) ≠c1996. | [publisher], ≠c |
| 1.6.12. | 260 | ≠a( ) Libraries Unlimited,  ≠c c1996. | [place] :  ≠b |
| 1.6.13. | 260 | ≠a Converse, La. :  ≠b Lewis Pub.,  ≠(d)c1990. | c |
| 1.6.14. | 260(0) | ≠a Gem, KS :  ≠b J.W. Pub. Co.,  ≠c c1982. | |
| 1.6.15. | 300 | ≠a 123 p. :  ≠(c) ill. ;  ≠c 22 cm. | b |
| 1.6.16. | 300 | ≠a 54 p. ;  ≠(b) 25 cm. | c |
| 1.6.17. | 300 | ≠(b) 2 v. ;  ≠c 26 cm. | a |
| 1.6.18. | 300 | ≠a 145 p. :  ≠ b maps, ill. ;  ≠c (1965-) | [# cm.] |
| 1.6.19. | (301) | ≠a 13 v. :  ≠b ill. ;  ≠c 25 cm. | 300 |
| 1.6.20. | 600(2)0 | ≠Babin, Lisa B. ≠q (Lisa Beth) | 1 |
| 1.6.21. | 650 (10) | ≠a Basketball  ≠x History | 0 |
| 1.6.22. | (650)  0 | ≠a Indiana  ≠x Description and travel. | 651 |
| 1.6.23. | (610) 20 | ≠a Art for New Artists Conference. | 611 |
| 1.6.24. | 651 0 | ≠(x) Alaska  ≠x Politics and government. | a |
| 1.6.25. | 650  0 | ≠a Automobiles  ≠(y) Maintenance and repair. | x |
| 1.6.26. | (651 00) | ≠a Bible  ≠v Commentaries. | 630 00 |
| 1.6.27. | 611 20 | ≠a International Film Festival  ≠(p) (1996) | d |
| 1.6.28. | 600(20) | ≠a Starr (Actress) | 00 |
| 1.6.29. | (653 7) | ≠a Mystery fiction. | 655 _7 |
| 1.6.30. | 650  0 | ≠(y) Twentieth century. | a |
| 1.6.31. | (651)20 | ≠a Chicago Bulls. | 610 |
| 1.6.32. | 630 00 | ≠(t) Bible. ≠p O.T. ≠p Psalms ≠v Commentaries. | a |

# Multiple Errors Exercise Answers

                                                        **q**

1.6.33.    100 1        ≠a Smith-Rosen, G. N. ≠(p) (Guy Ngo)

           **1**                             **b**

1.6.34.    110(2)       ≠a Many (La.). ≠(c) Mayor.

                   **a**                   **d**

1.6.35.    100 1        ≠(q) Smith, John Bob, ≠(y) 1901-1946.

           **2**                                                         **)**

1.6.36.    111(1)       ≠a Golf days ≠n (10th : ≠d 1990 ; ≠c Many (La.) ◯

           **1**                             **b**

1.6.37.    110(2)       ≠a Louisiana. ≠(a) Office of Marine Fisheries.

           **1**

1.6.38.    245(0)4     ≠a The tale of two kitties / ≠c by Mama Cat.

           **1**         **a**

1.6.39.    245(0)0     ≠(b) Dogs : ≠b a long tale / ≠c compiled by John Reeder.

         **5**   **4**                         **c**

1.6.40.    24(0) 1(0)   ≠a The sound and the fury / ≠(b) Ralph Nader.

               **4**

1.6.41.    245 1(5)   ≠a Les miserables / ≠ c illustrated by Pablo Picasso.

           **5**                          **/**   **c**

1.6.42.    24(6)14     ≠a The soccer defeat (:) ≠(b) by the Boston Jets.

                               **[publisher]**   **c**

1.6.43.    260 (0)     ≠a New York : ≠b (Milwaukee), ≠(b) c1946,(≠c) 1982.

         **0**               **[La.] [blank]**     **[La.]**   **b**         **c**

1.6.44.    26(1)       ≠a Many◯ ; ≠(a) Shreveport◯ : ≠(a) Reeves, ≠(a) c1996.

                   **≠a**                  **c**   **1963**

1.6.45.    260        ◯ New York : ≠b Viking, ≠(b) (1693).

                   **New York**     **Viking Press,**   *[date]*

1.6.46.    260        ≠a (Viking Press) : ≠b (New York;) ≠c (28 cm.)

                   **a**                  **b**               **c**

1.6.47.    260        ≠(x) Baton Rouge : ≠(a) Ferguson Frolics, ≠(y) c1992.

       **[blank]**            **:**   **b**               **c 21 cm.**

1.6.48.    300 (1)    ≠a 2 v.(;) ≠(a) ill., maps, ports ; ≠(b) (8 in.)

|        |         | **0** | **1 v. (various pagings)** | **c** |
|--------|---------|-------|----------------------------|-------|
| 1.6.49. | 30①   |       | ≠a (x, 145, vi, 632, ix, 15 p.) ; ≠(b) 22 cm. |

**c** **22 x 28 cm.**

1.6.50.   300     ≠a 92 p. : ≠b col. ill., facsims. ; ≠(z) (28 x 22 cm.)

**260**     ≠a [S.l. : ≠b s.n., ≠c 1995].

1.6.51.   (300)     ( [S.l.] : ≠b [s.n.], ≠c [1995]. )

**q**     **d**

1.6.52.   600   10     ≠a Smith, J. B.  ≠(x) (John Bob),  ≠(y) 1952-

**2**

1.6.53.   610 ① 0     ≠a Colorado Rodeo Association.

**2**     **≠ n(**     **c**

1.6.54.   611 ① 0     ≠a Lutcher Rodeo Days ( ≠a ) 1st : ≠d 1996 ; ≠(b) Lutcher, La.)

**1**

1.6.55.   65① 0     ≠a Sabine Parish (La.)

**x**     **and travel.**

1.6.56.   651   0     ≠a Rhode Island  ≠(z) Description (.)

**x**     **≠y**

1.6.57.   650   0     ≠a Cherokee Indians  ≠(y) History (,) 18th century.

**5**  **[blank]**     **[blank]**     **v**

1.6.58.   6①0 ① 0     ≠a Jeremiah  ≠(x) (Fictitious character) ≠(x) Fiction.

**5**     **(Fictitious character)**

1.6.59.   6①0   0     ≠a F'lar ( , ≠q of Pern, ≠c Dragonrider.)

**610 10**     **.**

1.6.60.   (651 0)     ≠a Utah ◯ ≠b Office of Tourism.

**3**     **. [delete subheading]**

1.6.61.   600 ① 0     ≠a Jones family ( ≠x Genealogy. )

**1**     **. [delete subheading]**

1.6.62.   600 ② 0     ≠a Smith, Robbie ( , ≠x Biography. )

**1**     **(La.)**     **.**

1.6.63.   610 ② 0     ≠a Baton Rouge ( , Lousiana ) ( : ) ≠b Mayor.

**a**     **. ≠p**     **≠p**

1.6.64.   630 00     ≠(t) Bible (,) N.T. (,) Matthew.

**1.6.65.   (12) errors**

                                                        **d**

100  1             ≠a Smith, James D.,  ≠ⓒ 1956-

        **0**

245  1④        ≠a Dogs of the world /  ≠c by Jim Smith, Jr.

                          **1st ed.**

250               ≠a ⟨First edition.⟩

                        **New York**

260               ≠a ⟨N.Y.⟩:  ≠b Viking Press,  ≠c c1995.

                         **:**      **b**      **;**     **cm.**

300               ≠a ix, 256 p. ⟨;⟩  ≠ⓒ col. ill.⟨,⟩  ≠c⟨c1995.⟩

                    **≠a**                **[blank ]**

440  0        ⟨≠t⟩ Animals of the world⟨.⟩

                         **i**

500               ≠a Includes ⟨I⟩ndex.

                       **v**

650  0        ≠a Dogs  ≠ⓩ Encyclopedias.

**1.6.66.   (12) errors**

        **1**                   **b**

110 ②         ≠a Louisiana.  ≠ⓟ State Records Office.

        **5**                        **/**

24⓪10      ≠a Registry of state lands ⟨:⟩  ≠c Louisiana State Records Office.

250               ≠a 1996 ed.

                        **b**          **c**

260               ≠a Baton Rouge :  ≠ⓒ The Office,  ≠ⓑ 1996.

                            **c**

300               ≠a 1 v. (various pagings) ;  ≠ⓑ 28 cm.

500               ≠a Cover title.

        **0**         **a**

50④           ≠ⓒ Includes index.

                        **v**

651  0        ≠a Louisiana  ≠ⓧ Registers.

|   |   | **z** |
|---|---|---|
| 650   0 | | ≠a Land use  ≠⊙Louisiana. |

***Delete this whole line—it is a duplicate of the 110 field.***

⟮710 2  ≠a Louisiana.  ≠b State Records Office.⟯

### 1.6.67. (19) errors

| | **0** | **a** |
|---|---|---|
| 1①0 1 | | ≠ⓒRobb, Randall R. |

| | **1** | ≠**a** | **/** |
|---|---|---|---|
| 245 ⓪4 | | ◯The archer looses an arrow ⟮:⟯ ≠ c by Randall R. Robb and Sturgis S. Stubbs. |

**[blank]**

246 30    ≠i Title on spine:  ≠a Into the air⟮.⟯

≠**a 1**

250    ⟮≠1⟯st ed.

**a**    **,**

260    ⓟNew York, N.Y. :  ≠b Archery International ⟮;⟯ ≠c c2003.

300    ≠a 540 p. ;  ≠c 18 cm.

**a**

440   0    ≠ⓣSoldiery

| **5**   **7** | | ≠**2 gsafd** |
|---|---|---|
| 65⓪ ⓪ | | ≠a Horror stories.◯ |

| **5**   **7** | **a**   **Historical** | ≠**2 gsafd** |
|---|---|---|
| 65① ⓪ | | ≠ⓑ⟮Medieval⟯ fiction. ◯ |

**1**

700②    ≠a Stubbs, Sturgis S.

### 1.6.68. (22) errors

| **1** | | **.** ≠**b** |
|---|---|---|
| 110② | | ≠a Wisconsin◯Library of the Arts. |

| **0** | **a** | **b** |
|---|---|---|
| 245 1④ | ≠ⓣInventory control at the Library of the Arts :  ≠ⓒa manual | |

**c**

of procedures /  ≠ⓑ by the staff of the Wisconsin Library of the Arts.

**2004**

260    ≠a Madison, Wisc. :  ≠ b Library of the Arts,  ≠c⟮2040⟯.

        **[blank/blank]   leaves         c   28 cm.**

300 ⑴⑴        ≠a 25 ①  : ≠b ill. ;  ≠ⓑ ⟨11 in.⟩

        **[blank/blank]  bibliographical references and index.**

50⓪ ⑽        ≠a  Includes⟨index and bibliography⟩ .

        **1    1**                                                                                                                              **v**

6⑸0⓪0        ≠a Wisconsin. ≠ b Library of the Arts  ≠ⓧ  Handbooks, manuals, etc.

     **[blank]              [blank]**

650⓪0        ≠a Art⟨.⟩  ≠x Preservation.

     **[blank]           a**

650①0        ≠ⓧ  Books ≠x Repair.

*Delete this entire field. It is a duplicate of the 110 field.*

⟨710 2  ≠a Wisconsin Library of the Arts.⟩

### 1.6.69. (13) errors

      **1    1**                                                     .

1⓪0②        ≠a Michigan◯ ≠b Dept. of Highways.

245 10        ≠a Michigan highways.

       **6           ≠a  Lansing**

2⑸0        Ⓐ ⟨Lansin⟩ (Mich.) :  ≠b Dept. of Highways,  ≠c 1852-

               **a          ≠b              ≠c**

300        ≠ Ⓥv. : ⓑill., maps ; ⓒ28 cm.

321        ≠a Annual

362 0        ≠a Vol. 1, no. 1- (September 1852)-

            **a**

500        ≠ⓠ Title from cover.

   **1              a              v**

65⓪ 0        ≠ⓧ Michigan ≠ⓧ Periodicals.

### 1.6.70. (11) errors

    **1              a                  b**

110②        ≠ⓧ Philadelphia (Pa.). ≠ⓟ City Council.

    **5    4**

24⑹ 1⓪        ≠a The early history of Philadelphia :  ≠b from its founding to 1900.

        **[Asterisk]**

250        ≠aⓧ ed.

260      ≠a Philadelphia, Pa. : ≠b City Council, ≠c 1925.

                           **p.**

300      ≠a xix, 312 p., [16 (pages)] of plates : ≠b ill., maps, ports. ; ≠c 28 cm.

    **1**         **a**             **(Pa.)**                               **.**

65(0) 0      ≠(b) Philadelphia(, Pennsylvania) ≠x History(and description.)

## 1.6.71. (16) errors

   **100 1**         **a**             **(Albert George)**

(245 1 0)      ≠(q) Milne, A. G. ≠q (Albert George.)

        **4**                **Spain**            **/**

245 1 (0)      ≠a The plane in (Spane) mainly falls (;) ≠c A.G. Milne.

    **0**             **ed.**

25(1)      ≠a 16th (edition)

         **New York : ≠ b**            **c**

260      ≠a ( ) Little House Press, ≠(d) c1992.

             **p.**     **b**         **≠cm.**

300      ≠a xxxviii, 24(pages): ≠(c) ill., maps ; ≠c (c1992.)

   **0**    **0**          **z**

65(1) (1)      ≠a Aircraft ≠(x) Spain.

## 1.6.72. (17) errors

   **0**    **1 _** 

1(1) 0 (_ 0)      ≠a Gargantua, Draconus.

    **5 10**                         **c**

24(0)      ≠a My life as the Black Dragon / ≠(b) Draconus Gargantua.

    **6**                        ***[Publisher], ≠c***

2(5)0      ≠a Munich, Germany : ≠b ( ) c1994.

       **a**      **:**     **ill. geneal.**      **≠c**

300      ≠(A) 365 p(;) ≠b(illus.) ,(gen.) tables ;( ) 27 cm.

    **0 _**     **≠**       **[blank]**

490(_ 0)      (/) a My life series (.)

    **0**    **10**        **Draconus**

6(5)0(0 _)      ≠a Gargantua,(Draconius .)

**1.6.73. (19) errors**

**700  [blank]**
(100) 1 (0)      ≠a Chan, Lois Mai.

**5  00       a                        classification  :**
24(4) (14)    ≠(b) Dewey decimal (classfication) (/) ≠b a practical guide /

≠                              .

(◆) c Lois Mai Chan ... [et. al.] (○)

**0                        rev.**
25(5)      ≠a 2nd ed. (Revised)

**0                          , N.Y.**
26(6)      ≠a Albany (          ) :  ≠b Forest Press, ≠c 1996.

**a           ;    c  22 cm.**
300       ≠ (A) 322 p.(○) ≠(b) (8 ½ in.)

**4            Includes**
50(0)      ≠a (Contains) bibliographical references and index.

650  0     ≠a Classification, Dewey decimal.

# 2.1.   *AACR2R* Areas Exercise Answers

2.1.1.     x.1

2.1.2.     x.4

2.1.3.     x.7

2.1.4.     x.8

2.1.5.     x.0

2.1.6.     x.2

2.1.7.     x.9

2.1.8.     x.5

2.1.9.     x.3

2.1.10.    x.6

2.1.11.    x.10

2.1.12.    x.11

2.1.13.    General rules ; Edition area

2.1.14.    Cartographic materials ; Publication, distribution area

2.1.15.    Electronic resources ; Title and statement of responsibility area

2.1.16.    Three-dimensional artefacts and realia ; General rules

2.1.17.    Sound recordings ; Material-specific details area

2.1.18.     Graphic materials ; Physical description area

2.1.19.     Books, pamphlets and printed sheets ; Series area

2.1.20.     Music ; Standard number and terms of availability area

2.1.21.     Manuscripts ; Notes area

2.1.22.     Microforms; Physical description area

2.1.23.     Motion pictures and videorecordings ; Supplementary items

# 2.2.   *AACR2R* General Exercise Answers

2.2.1.     Michael Gorman and Paul W. Winkler.

2.2.2.     No. Summary of rule revisions since 1998.

2.2.3.     x.0B [zero B]

2.2.4.     x.0D [zero D]

2.2.5.     x.0C [zero C]

2.2.6.     Transcribe the inaccuracy or misspelling as it appears in the item. Follow that with either *[sic]* or *i.e.,[corrected information]*. You can also supply a missing letter or letters in square brackets, such as *T[h]e*.

2.2.7.     x.0F [zero F]

2.2.8.     x.0H [zero H]

2.2.9.     1.0B [1.zero B]

2.2.10.    No. Rule 25.1A.

2.2.11.    Roman script. Rule 25.2D1.

2.2.12.    25.2C

2.2.13.    No. *AACR2R* contains the rules for descriptive cataloging, not subject cataloging. The only rules governing subjects are those in Part II, which tell you how to formulate names.

2.2.14.    1.1C.

2.2.15.    No.

2.2.16.    *The Chicago Manual of Style* is the authority. Rule 0.11 [zero.11].

2.2.17.    No. The examples only illuminate the provisions of the rule to which they are attached. They are illustrative, not prescriptive. Rule 0.14.

2.2.18.    *The Library of Congress Rule Interpretations (LCRI).*

2.2.19.    Both. *AACR2R* gives rules for the description of materials being cataloged, not how they are input into a computer or typed on a catalog card.

2.2.20.    It means that a statement to which it applies must be a formal statement found in one of the prescribed sources of information in areas 1 and 2. Rule 0.8.

2.2.21.    No.

2.2.22.    Not if they are designated as **optional**. You may do so to avoid conflicts in the future.

2.2.23.   No, they don't. If no specific rule applies, use the general rule from Chapter 1.

2.2.24.   Yes. Rule 21.1B1.

# 2.3.   *AACR2R*, Part I Exercise Answers

2.3.1.   The title page, or if there is no title page, the source on or within the publication that substitutes for the title page.

2.3.2.   The part of the item supplying the most complete information. It may be the cover, half title page, caption, colophon, running title, or other part.

2.3.3.   Allowable places from which information can be used in various areas of the bibliographical record, i.e., chief source or other places for formats other than books.

2.3.4.   No. You are told to use the general statement given in Rule 1.0F.

2.3.5.   Preceding the information.

2.3.6.   For an Oriental, non-Roman script publication, if the colophon contains full bibliographic information. Rule 2.0B1.

2.3.7.   Any source.

2.3.8.   2.0D, 2.0E, 2.0F, 2.0G, 2.0H

# 2.4.   Personal Names (Chapter 22) Exercise Answers

2.4.1.   *AACR2R* rule: 22.15A
Read, Miss.

2.4.2.   *AACR2R* rule: 22.11A
Grandfather Fortnight.

2.4.3.   *AACR2R* rule: 22.11B
Sam, Uncle.

2.4.4.   *AACR2R* rule: 22.10A
D. de F.

2.4.5.   *AACR2R* rule: 22.8A1
Pliny, the Elder.

2.4.6.   *AACR2R* rule: 22.13B
Catherine, Saint, of Genoa.

2.4.7.   *AACR2R* rule: 22.5C3
Smythe-Hetherington, Henri.

2.4.8.   *AACR2R* rule: 22.16A3
Marie Antoinette, consort of Louis, XVI, of France.

2.4.9.     *AACR2R* rule: 22.3C1
           Marsilius, of Padua.

2.4.10.    *AACR2R* rule: 22.6A1
           Byron, George Gordon Byron, Baron.

2.4.11.    *AACR2R* rule: 22.9A
           Cicero, Marcus Tullius.

2.4.12.    *AACR2R* rule: 22.5C4
           Tall Chief, Maria.

2.4.13.    *AACR2R* rule: 22.16B1
           Leo XIII, Pope.

2.4.14.    *AACR2R* rule: 22.18A
           Wells, H. G. (Herbert George)

2.4.15.    *AACR2R* rule: 22.11A
           Buffalo Bob.

2.4.16.    *AACR2R* rule: 22.2B1
           Carroll, Lewis.

2.4.17.    *AACR2R* rule: 22.2B3
           Michaels, Barbara.

2.4.18.    *AACR2R* rule: 22.1A
           H. D.

2.4.19.    *AACR2R* rule: 22.16A2
           Richard I, King of England.

2.4.20.    *AACR2R* rule: 22.5F1
           Hohenzollern, Franz Joseph, Fürst von.

2.4.21.    *AACR2R* rule: 22.5E1
           MacGruff, Frank.

2.4.22.    *AACR2R* rule: 22.15A
           Jones, Nurse.

2.4.23.    *AACR2R* rule: 22.19B1
           Smith, John, Ship captain.

## 2.5.  Corporate Bodies (Chapter 24), Exercise Set 1 Answers

2.5.1.   Alabama. Commission on Certification of Social Workers.

2.5.2.   First Presbyterian Church (Boise, Idaho)

2.5.3.   Montana.

2.5.4.   Governor's Conference on Mental Disabilities (3rd : 1957 : Ames, Iowa)

2.5.5.   University of Mississippi. Coastal Resources Section.

2.5.6.   Catholic Church. Pope (1878-1903 : Leo XIII)

2.5.7.   Republican Party (La.). State Committee.

2.5.8.   West Baton Rouge Genealogical Society.

2.5.9.   Freemasons. Grand Lodge. (Lafayette, La.).

2.5.10.  United States. Congress. House of Representatives. Committee on Public Health. Subcommittee on the Federal-Aid Adult Daycare Program.

2.5.11.  Nebraska. Supreme Court.

2.5.12.  Maine Library Association. Technical Services Interest Group.

2.5.13.  Kidd (Ship)

2.5.14.  Architectural Students Forum (University of New Orleans)

2.5.15.  Mississippi. Pearl River Administration.

2.5.16.  Jesuits.

2.5.17.  Episcopal Church. Diocese of Western Louisiana.

2.5.18.  University of Louisiana, Lafayette. Center for Louisiana Studies.

2.5.19.  KEEL (Radio station : Shreveport, La.)

2.5.20.  Las Vegas (N.M.). Assessor.

2.5.21.  Presbyterian Church (U.S.). National Council.

2.5.22.  Monitor (Ship)

2.5.23.  Holy Jesus Church (Brooklyn, New York, N.Y. : Baptist)

2.5.24.  United States. Congress. House of Representatives.

2.5.25.  United States. Army. Infantry Division, 16th.

2.5.26.  United States. Naval Air Corps.

2.5.27.  Louisiana. Constitutional Convention (1989).

2.5.28.  Utah. Department of Revenue.

2.5.29.  Rice Festival (5th : Cameron, La.)

2.5.30.  Red River Compact Administration.

2.5.31.  Cheniere Caminada Delta Management Program.

2.5.32.  Chile. Embassy (U.S.)

2.5.33.  United States. President (2002- : Bush)

2.5.34.  Kaw Valley Film & Video.

# Corporate Bodies (Chapter 22), Exercise Set 2 Answers

2.5.35.   *AACR2R* rule 24.20C1
South Bend (Ind.). Mayor.

2.5.36.   *AACR2R* rule 24.11
WJBO (Radio station : Baton Rouge, La.)

2.5.37.   *AACR2R* rule 24.4C1
Terrebonne Genealogical Society.

2.5.38.   *AACR2R* rule 24.5C4
Danley (Ship)

2.5.39.   *AACR2R* rule 24.13
Louisiana State University (Baton Rouge, La.). Center for Wetland Resources.

2.5.40.   *AACR2R* rule 24.13
Catholic Church. Pope (1978- : John Paul II)

2.5.41.   *AACR2R* rule 24.4C2
Republican Party (Me.)

2.5.42.   *AACR2R* rule 24.16A
Democratic Party (N.Y.). State Committee.

2.5.43.   *AACR2R* rule 24.2D
NATO.

2.5.44.   *AACR2R* rule 24.7B
Governor's Conference on Physical Disabilities (2nd : 1978 : New Orleans, La.)

2.5.45.   *AACR2R* rule 24.21C
United States. Congress. House of Representatives. Committee on Public Works.
Special Subcommittee on the Federal-Aid Highway Program.

2.5.46.   *AACR2R* rule 24.18
Mississippi. Environmental Protection Agency.

2.5.47.   *AACR2R* rule 24.9A
Freemasons. Grand Lodge (Baton Rouge, La.).

2.5.48.   *AACR2R* rule 24.12
Paul M. Hebert Law Center.

2.5.49.   *AACR2R* rule 24.4C7
Tiger Tales Club (University of New Orleans)

2.5.50.   *AACR2R* rule 24.27C2
Catholic Church. Louisiana Diocese.

2.5.51.    *AACR2R* rule 24.3D1
Poor Clares.

2.5.52.    *AACR2R* rule 24.23A
Louisiana. Supreme Court.

2.5.53.    *AACR2R* rule 24.20B
United States. President (1961-1963 : Kennedy)

2.5.54.    *AACR2R* rule 24.10B
First Baptist Church (Big Wood, La.)

2.5.55.    *AACR2R* rule 24.19
Louisiana. Bureau of Environmental Health.

2.5.56.    *AACR2R* rule 24.24A1
United States. Army Air Corps.

2.5.57.    *AACR2R* rule 24.4B
F4 Phantom (Jet plane)

2.5.58.    *AACR2R* rule 24.27A1
Episcopal Church (U.S.). National Council.

2.5.59.    *AACR2R* rule 24.21A
United States. Congress. Senate.

2.5.60.    *AACR2R* rule 24.10
All Saints Church (Manhattan, N.Y. : Catholic)

2.5.61.    *AACR2R* rule 24.22B
Louisiana. Constitutional Convention (1973)

2.5.62.    *AACR2R* rule 24.24A1
United States. Army. Infantry Division, 25th.

2.5.63.    *AACR2R* rule 24.8
Shrimp Festival (3rd : Houma, La.)

2.5.64.    *AACR2R* rule 24.18
Louisiana. Department of Culture, Recreation and Tourism.

2.5.65.    *AACR2R* rule 24.15A
Sabine River Compact Administration.

2.5.66.    *AACR2R* rule 24.18
Mongolia. Embassy (Great Britain)

2.5.67.    *AACR2R* rule 24.17
Kisatchie-Delta Regional Management Program.

2.5.68.    *AACR2R* rule 24.5C1
Coronet Film and Video.

# 2.6. Geographic Names, Exercise Set 1 Answers

2.6.1.    Paris (France)

2.6.2.    Broadmoor (Shreveport, La.)

2.6.3.    Beijing (China)

2.6.4.    Naples (Italy)

2.6.5.    Ontario

2.6.6.    Fort Erie (Ontario)

2.6.7.    York (England)

2.6.8.    Ulaanbaatar (Mongolia)

2.6.9.    Linwood (Bartow County, Ga.)

2.6.10.   Linwood (Walker County, Ga.)

2.6.11.   Kansas City (Mo.)

## Geographic Names Exercise Set 2 Answers

2.6.12.   *AACR2R* rule 23.4C2
         Yellow Creek (Sask.)

2.6.13.   *AACR2R* rule 23.4E
         Bonn (Germany)

2.6.14.   *AACR2R* rule 23.5A
         Pôrto Mendes (Brazil)

2.6.15.   *AACR2R* rule 23.4D2
         Strathaven (Scotland)

2.6.16.   *AACR2R* rule 23.4C1
         Queensland

2.6.17.   *AACR2R* rule 23.2B1
         Zhangmu (China)

2.6.18.   *AACR2R* rule 23.4C2
         Alice Springs (N.T.)

2.6.19.   *AACR2R* rule 23.4E
         Lhasa (China)

2.6.20.   *AACR2R* rule 23.5A
         Nuevo Laredo (Mexico)

2.6.21.   *AACR2R* rule 23.4D2
         Bushmills (Northern Ireland)

2.6.22.   *AACR2R* rule 23.4C1
Pecos Wilderness (New Mexico)

2.6.23.   *AACR2R* rule 23.2B1
Puerta Vallerta (Mexico)

2.6.24.   *AACR2R* rule 23.4C2
Omaha (Neb.)

2.6.25.   *AACR2R* rule 23.4E
Kathmandu (Nepal)

2.6.26.   *AACR2R* rule 23.4D2
Llanelly (Wales)

2.6.27.   *AACR2R* rule 23.5A
Ciudad Hidalgo (Mexico)

2.6.28.   *AACR2R* rule 23.4C1
Yukon

# 2.7.   Choice of Access Points Exercise Answers

2.7.1.   The choice of access points, or headings, under which a bibliographic description is entered in a catalog.

2.7.2.   Chief source of information, or its substitute.

2.7.3.   Compiler, editor, illustrator, translator.

2.7.4.   Abbreviated.

2.7.5.   No, other designations can be added as instructed in particular rules.

2.7.6.   The person chiefly responsible for the creation of the intellectual or artistic content of a work.

2.7.7.   21.1B2

2.7.8.   A work emanates from a corporate body if it is issued by that body, or has been caused to be issued by that body, or if it originated with that body.

2.7.9.   Treat it as if it doesn't.

2.7.10.   Treat it as if no corporate body were involved, and make added entries for prominently named corporate bodies.

2.7.11.   Yes. Enter a work under title if (a) the personal author is unknown or diffuse, (b) the work does not emanate from a corporate body, (c) it is produced under editorial direction, (d) it emanates from a corporate body but does not fall into any categories in 21.1B2, or (e) it is accepted as sacred scripture by a religious group.

2.7.12.   No.

2.7.13.    Consider that the title has a minor change and make appropriate notes for the changes.

2.7.14.    Make a new record.

2.7.15.    Make a new record.

2.7.16.    Enter it under the corporate heading for the official.

2.7.17.    Enter it under the personal name heading, not the corporate name heading.

2.7.18.    Enter it under title main entry. Do not make an added entry for the symbols.

2.7.19.    (a) Works produced by two or more persons, (b) works for which different persons have prepared separate contributions, (c) works consisting of an exchange between two or more persons, such as correspondence or debates, (d) works falling into one or more of the categories given in Rule 21.1B2, (e) works consisting or a combination of personal and corporate authors.

2.7.20.    When there are more than three authors.

2.7.21.    Only the first is given in the statement of responsibility, and is traced as added entry. The others are not named at all.

2.7.22.    The one named first in the chief source of information.

2.7.23.    Each edition is entered under the person entered first on the chief source of information, and the other is traced as an added entry.

2.7.24.    Use the pseudonym as the main entry.

2.7.25.    Enter it under the heading appropriate to the new work if the modification has substantially changed the nature and content of the original, or if the medium of expression has changed.

2.7.26.    Enter it under the heading appropriate to the original.

2.7.27.    Enter it under the name of the adapter.

2.7.28.    Enter it under the heading appropriate for the original work.

2.7.29.    Enter it under the heading appropriate for the original work.

2.7.30.    To provide access to bibliographic descriptions in addition to the access provided by the main entry heading.

2.7.31.    Persons, corporate bodies, and titles.

2.7.32.    Yes.

2.7.33.    No.

2.7.34.    Not necessarily. There are separate rules dealing with analytical entries, and Rule 21.30M1 states that analytical entries would be made according to the policy of the individual institution.

2.7.35.    No.

# 2.8. Uniform Titles Exercise Answers

2.8.1.    It is enclosed in square brackets.

2.8.2.    Uniform titles appear in 130 or 240 fields; titles proper appear in 245 fields. Uniform titles have no initial articles unless the uniform title is to file under that article; titles proper may or may not have initial articles.

2.8.3.    No.

2.8.4.    Romanize it according to the table for that language adopted by the cataloging agency.

2.8.5.    Use the title of the edition published in the home country of the cataloging agency.

2.8.6.    English, French, German, Spanish, Russian.

2.8.7.    The language of the edition first received by the library.

2.8.8.    If there is only one edition in the library, you may choose not to use a uniform title, but instead put a note about the availability of other editions in other languages.

2.8.9.    Use a well-established English title, if there is one. If not, use the Latin title. If there is neither English or Latin, use the Greek title.

2.8.10.   Add in parentheses an appropriate explanatory word, brief phrase, or other designation. [Example: "Charlemagne (Emperor)" and "Charlemagne (Play)". In an automated system, the first would be placed in a 100 field, and the second in a 130 field.]

2.8.11.   Add parenthetical phrases of versions [for example, Southern version or Northern version], or add dates.

2.8.12.   Put the language of the item being cataloged after a full stop following the uniform title. [Example: Beowulf. French.]

2.8.13.   No. Do not add the name of the language to the uniform title.

2.8.14.   Add the name of the modern language followed by the name of the early form in parentheses. [Example: English (Middle English)]

2.8.15.   Add both languages after the uniform title, the original language named second.

2.8.16.   Use the following preference table: English, French, German, Spanish, Russian, other languages in alphabetic order of their names in English.

2.8.17.   After the uniform title use "Polyglot".

2.8.18.   Use the uniform title for the whole work followed by "Selections", after a full stop.

2.8.19.   Use the uniform title "Works".

2.8.20.   Use "Selections".

2.8.21.   Use one of the following collective titles: Correspondence, Essays, Novels, Plays, Poems, Prose works, Short stories. Speeches.

2.8.22.   Use the appropriate specific collective title, such as Posters or Fragments.

2.8.23.   Use "Laws, etc.".

2.8.24.   Use in this order of preference: (a) the official short title or citation title, (b) an unofficial short title or citation title used in legal literature, (c) the official title of the enactment, or (d) any other official designation such as the number or date.

2.8.25.   Add the year of promulgation of the original acts.

2.8.26.   Use "Treaties, etc." followed by the name of the other party.

2.8.27.   Use "Treaties, etc." by itself.

2.8.28.   Use the title by which it is most commonly identified in English-language reference sources dealing with the group to which the scripture belongs.

2.8.29.   Use Bible followed by the testament [O.T. or N.T.]; the book; the number if it is one of a numbered sequence of the same name such as Corinthians, 1$^{st}$; the chapter (in roman numerals); and the verse (in Arabic numerals).

2.8.30.   Bible. [testament]. [special group]. Example: Bible. N.T. Catholic Epistles.

2.8.31.   Bible. O.T. Apocrypha.

2.8.32.   Use the commonly identified title.

2.8.33.   Yes, but the first is the main entry and the second is a uniform title added entry.

2.8.34.   Use the uniform title followed by: [language] of the item being cataloged, [version], [selections], and [year].

2.8.35.   Enter it as a subheading of Talmud or Talmud Yerushalmi, as appropriate.

2.8.36.   *Encyclopaedia Judaica.*

2.8.37.   Enter them as a subheading of Vedas. If the item is a particular version, add the name of the version in parentheses.

# 3.2.   References Exercise Answers

## Personal names, *See From* references

| 3.2.1. | 400 1 | Jones, Seymour Rochambaud. UF Jones, Seymour Rochambaud |
|---|---|---|
| 3.2.2. | 400 1 | Faust, Frederick, ≠d 1892-1944. UF Faust, Frederick, 1892-1944 |
| 3.2.3. | 400 1 | Boynton, Janice Hendricks UF Boynton, Janice Hendricks |
| 3.2.4. | 400 1 | Rice, Katherine. UF Rice, Katherine |

## Personal names, *See Also* references

| 3.2.5 | 500 1 | Carroll, Lewis, ≠d 1832-1898.<br>SA Carroll, Lewis, 1832-1898 |

## Corporate names, *See From* references

| 3.2.6. | 410 1 | Louisiana. ≠b Dept. of Culture, Recreation and Tourism  ≠ b Office of State Library.<br>UF Louisiana. Dept. of Culture, Recreation and Tourism. Office of State Library |
| 3.2.7. | 410 1 | Kentucky. ≠b Vocational Education Section.<br>UF Kentucky. Vocational Education Section |
| 3.2.8. | 410 2 | BNA.<br>UF BNA |
| 3.2.9. | 410 1 | United States. ≠b Interior, Department of the.<br>UF United States. Interior, Department of the |

## Corporate names, *See Also* references

| 3.2.10. | 510 2 | Louisiana State University (Baton Rouge, La.)<br>SA Louisiana State University (Baton Rouge, La.) |
| 3.2.11. | 510 2 | Tulane University. ≠b Newcomb College.<br>SA Tulane University. Newcomb College |

## Subject headings, *See From* references

| 3.2.12. | 450 0 | Baby sitting.<br>UF Baby sitting. |
| 3.2.13. | 450 0 | Homosexuals, Male.<br>UF Homosexuals, Male |
| 3.2.14 | 450 0 | Police officers.<br>UF Police officers |

## Subject headings, *See Also* references

| 3.2.15. | 550 0 | Cookery ≠z Louisiana.<br>RT Cookery -- Louisiana |
| 3.2.16. | 550 0 | Snakes<br>NT Snakes |
| 3.2.17. | 550 0 | Indians of North America<br>BT Indians of North America |

3.2.18.  550 0  Escalators
RT Escalators

## Geographical headings, *See From* references

3.2.19.  450 0  Kola Peninsula (R.S.F.S.R.)
UF Kola Peninsula (R.S.F.S.R.)

3.2.20.  451 0  St. John the Baptist Parish (La.)
UF St. John the Baptist Parish (La.)

3.2.21.  451 0  Ontonagon County, Mich.
UF Ontonagon County, Mich.

3.2.22.  451 0  Commonwealth of Pennsylvania
UF Commonwealth of Pennsylvania

## Geographical names, *See Also* references

3.2.23.  551 0  Washington D.C. Regional Area.
SA Washington D.C. Regional Area

3.2.24.  551 0  French Quarter (New Orleans, La.) ≠x History.
NT French Quarter (New Orleans, La.) ≠x History

3.2.25.  551 0  New York (N.Y.)
BT New York (N.Y.)

# 3.3.  Authority Control, Exercise Set 1 Answers

3.3.1.  150  ≠a Power lawn mowers ≠x Maintenance and repair ≠v Handbooks, manuals, etc.
450  ≠a Power lawnmowers
450  ≠a Lawnmowers, Power
550  ≠a Garden equipment
670  ≠a Ferguson, G. Repairing your power lawnmower, c2004.

3.3.2.  151  ≠a Driskoll, Mount
451  ≠a Mount Driskoll
451  ≠a Mt. Driskoll
550  ≠a Mountains ≠z Louisiana
670  ≠a Lilly, J. Louisiana's highest peak, c1991.

3.3.3.  100 1 _  ≠a Jaques, Thomas F.
400 1 _  ≠a Jaques, Tom.
550  ≠a State librarians ≠v Biography.
670  ≠a His Autobiography of a State Librarian, c2001. ≠b t.p. (Thomas F. Jaques ; p. ii, Tom Jaques)

3.3.4.    110    1    ≠a Louisiana. ≠b Office of the Governor.

          410    1    ≠a Louisiana. ≠b Governor, Office of the.

          410    1    ≠ a Louisiana. ≠b Governor's Office.

          670         ≠a State of the state report, 1995, 1995.  ≠b t.p. (Louisiana Office of the Governor)

3.3.5.    150         ≠a Oliver, Gideon (Fictitious character)

          450         ≠a Gideon Oliver (Fictitious character)

          450         ≠a Skeleton Detective (Fictitious character)

          450         ≠a Professor Oliver (Fictitious character)

          670         ≠a Elkins, A. The dark place, 1987.

3.3.6.    100    1    ≠ a Lewis, Marvin W. ≠q (Marvin Wells),  ≠d 1964-

          400    0    ≠a Lewis, Marvin Wells, ≠d 1964-

          400    0    ≠a Lewis, Trey.

          670         ≠a His Indian artifacts of the Gulf Coast, c1998. ≠b t.p. (Marvin Wells Lewis) ; phone call to author (generally known as Trey; born in 1964)

# 3.4.    Authority Control (Header), Exercise Set 1 Answers

| | | | | | |
|---|---|---|---|---|---|
| 3.4.1. | 008 | na.acnndaabn | | a.aaa | d |
| 3.4.2. | 008 | na.acnndaabn | | a.aaa | d |
| 3.4.3. | 008 | na.acnndaabn | | a.aaa | d |
| 3.4.4. | 008 | na.acnndaabn | | a.aaa | d |
| 3.4.5. | 008 | na.acnndaabn | | a.aaa | d |
| 3.4.6. | 008 | na.acnndaabn | | l a.aaa | d |
| 3.4.7. | 008 | na.acnndaabn | | a.aaa | d |
| 3.4.8. | 008 | na.acnndaabn | | a.ana | d |
| 3.4.9. | 008 | na.acnndaabn | | a.ana | d |
| 3.4.10. | 008 | na.acnndaabn | | f a.ana | d |
| 3.4.11. | 008 | ia.acbndbabn | | a.ana | d |
| 3.4.12. | 008 | ia.acbndbabn | | a.ana | d |
| 3.4.13. | 008 | ia.acbndbabn | | a.ana | d |
| 3.4.14. | 008 | ia.acbndbabn | | a.ana | d |
| 3.4.15. | 008 | ia.acbndbabn | | a.ana | d |
| 3.4.16. | 008 | ia.acbndbabn | | a.ana | d |
| 3.4.17. | 008 | ia.acbndbabn | | a.ana | d |
| 3.4.18. | 008 | ia.acbndbabn | | a.ana | d |
| 3.4.19. | 008 | ia.acbndbabn | | a.ana | d |

3.4.20.    008 . . . . . . . .    ia.acbndbabn . . . . . . . . . . . . .    a.ana . . . . . . . .    d

3.4.21.    008 . . . . . . . .    na.acnabbban . . . . . . . . . . . . .    a.ana . . . . . . . .    d

3.4.22.    008 . . . . . . . .    na.acnabbban . . . . . . . . . . . . .    a.ana . . . . . . . .    d

3.4.23.    008 . . . . . . . .    na.acnabbban . . . . . . . . . . . . .    a.ana . . . . . . . .    d

3.4.24.    008 . . . . . . .    na.acnabbban . . . . . . . . . . . . .    a.ana . . . . . . . .    d

3.4.25.    008 . . . . . . . .    na.acnabbban . . . . . . . . . . . . .    a.ana . . . . . . . .    d

# Authority Control (Header), Exercise Set 2 Answers

3.4.26.    110 1    ≠a United States. ≠b Topographical Bureau
ARN: 302452

3.4.27.    651  0    ≠a Baton Rouge (La.) ≠v Maps
ARN: 288770 ; 4933824

3.4.28.    100 1    ≠a Smith, Joseph
ARN: 676289

3.4.29.    650     ≠a Art, American
ARN: 2032033

3.4.30.    651  0    ≠a Topeka (Kan.)
ARN: 379976

3.4.31.    650 0    ≠a Animals  ≠z Africa
ARN: 2018489 ; 2001892

3.4.32.    610 20    ≠a Hibernia Bank *[110 2 is also acceptable.]*
ARN: 5105601

3.4.33.    610 20    ≠a Alabama Museum of Natural History *[110 2 is also acceptable.]*
ARN: 107652

3.4.34.    611 20    ≠a Superbowl
ARN: 4904116

3.4.35.    830 0    ≠a Computer indexed marriage records
ARN: 1445099

3.4.36.    610 10    ≠a United States. ≠b President's Commission on Women's Issues
ARN: 4322120

3.4.37.    110 2    ≠a Paul M. Hebert Law Center
ARN: 846840

3.4.38.    110 1    ≠a Fletcher, Mary Dell
ARN: 1769084

3.4.39.     650 0          ≠a Fishing  ≠v Humor
                            ARN: 2160312 ; 4933814

3.4.40.     650 0          ≠a Crayfish  x Marketing
                            ARN: 2060223 ; 5100263

3.4.41.     651  0         ≠a Uluru-Kata Tjuta National Park (N.T.)
                            ARN: 2413086

3.4.42.     650 0          ≠a Fantasy fiction
                            ARN: 2151209

3.4.43.     610 10         ≠a United States. ≠b Navy ≠v Biography
                            ARN: 292099 ; 4933801

3.4.44.     650 0          ≠a Country music
                            ARN: 2056854

3.4.45.     650 0          ≠a Arithmetic ≠x Study and teaching (Primary)
                            ARN: 2030014 [or] 2029963 ; 5547901

3.4.46.     650 0          ≠a China  ≠x Description and travel
                            ARN: 323484 ; 4933831

3.4.47.     611 20         ≠a Masters Golf Tournament
                            ARN: 4532350

3.4.48.     651  0         ≠a Fort Bayard (N.M.) ≠v Maps
                            ARN: 3024900 ; 4933824

3.4.49.     651  0         ≠a Calcutta (India)
                            ARN: 431503

3.4.50.     651  0         ≠a Marrakech (Morocco)
                            ARN: 431503

3.4.51.     650 0          ≠a Wild and scenic rivers
                            ARN: 2101443

3.4.52.     100 1          ≠a Forbidden City (Beijing, China)
                            ARN: 2004052

3.4.53.     100 0          ≠a Alexander, ≠c the Great, ≠d 356-323 B.C.
                            ARN: 238252

3.4.54.     100 1          ≠a Diana, ≠c Princess of Wales, ≠d 1961-
                            ARN: 618798

3.4.55.     651  0         ≠a Outer space
                            ARN: 2104024

| 3.4.56. | 651 | 0 | ≠a Tbilisi (Georgia) |
| | | | ARN: 336341 |

| 3.4.57. | 650 | 0 | ≠a Fishing nets  ≠z Mekong River |
| | | | ARN: 2160436 ; 2012424 |

| 3.4.58. | 650 | 0 | ≠a Swamps  ≠z Florida |
| | | | ARN: 2161389 [or] 2161381 ; 287141 |

| 3.4.59. | 650 | 0 | ≠a Mountain guides (Persons)  ≠z Nepal |
| | | | ARN: 2039614 ; 323842 |

# 3.5.  Authority Control Creation, Exercise Answers

In the answers for these exercises the 040 field will be left blank because the answers will vary according to user.

**Corporate Names**

**3.5.1.**

| 008 | | | y y m m d d n a . a c n n d a a b n . . . . . . . . . . . a . a a a . . . . . d |
| 040 | | | ≠a _____  ≠c _____ |
| 110 | 0 | 2 | ≠a Westin Photographic Company. |
| 410 | 2 | | ≠a Westin Films. |
| 410 | 2 | | ≠a Westin Photographs. |
| 670 | | | ≠a Its Westin professional moving pictures and stills, c1983.  ≠b t.p. (Westin Photographic Company). |
| 670 | | | ≠a Smith, William Robert. A Westin history, c1993. ≠ b p. ii-iii (established in 1901 as Westin Films ; succeeded by Westin Photographs in 1918; became Westin Photographic Company in 1935. Began publishing in 1952.) |

**3.5.2.**

| 008 | | | y y m m d d n a . a c n n d a a b n . . . . . . . . . . a . a a a . . . . . d |
| 040 | | | ≠a _____  ≠c _____ |
| 110 | 1 | | ≠a Louisiana.  ≠b Department of Education. |
| 410 | 1 | | ≠a Louisiana.  ≠b Education, Department of. |
| 410 | 1 | | ≠a Louisiana. ≠ b State Department of Education. |
| 410 | 1 | | ≠a Louisiana.  ≠b State Department of Public Education. |
| 670 | | | ≠a Louisiana. Bureau of Minority Education. End-of-the-year report for minority education programs, 1984.  ≠b t.p. (Louisiana Department of Education); p. 2 (Louisiana State Department of Education). |

| 670 | ≠a Matt, Katherine. Louisiana history, 1966. ≠b p. 9 (State Department of Public Education). |

**3.5.3.**

| 008 | y y m m d d n a . a c n n d a a b n . . . . . . . . . . . a . a a a . . . . . d |
| 040 | ≠a _____ ≠c _____ |
| 110 2 | ≠a Minton-Shropshire Porcelain Company. |
| 410 0 | ≠a Minton Porcelain Company. |
| 410 0 | ≠a Shropshire Porcelain Company. |
| 510 2 | ≠a Minton-Shropshire Unlimited. |
| 670 | ≠a Its Pseudo-porcelains, 1895. ≠b (Minton-Shropshire Porcelain Company Limited). |
| 670 | ≠a William, Teal. The history of the Minton and Shropshire Companies, 1996. (Firm founded in 1832 as Minton-Shropshire Porcelain Company Limited; used "Minton Porcelain Company", "Shropshire Porcelain Company" and "M-S P" marks on various manufactures during 1835-1839; renamed Minton-Shropshire Unlimited in 1840). |

**3.5.3.**

| 008 | y y m m d d n a . a c n n d a a b n . . . . . . . . . . . a . a a a . . . . . d |
| 040 | ≠a _____ ≠c _____ |
| 110 2 | ≠a Minton-Shropshire Unlimited. |
| 410 0 | ≠a Minton Porcelain Company. |
| 410 0 | ≠a Shropshire Porcelain Company. |
| 510 2 | ≠a Minton-Shropshire Porcelain Company. |
| 670 | ≠a William, Teal. The history of the Minton and Shropshire Companies, 1996. (Firm founded in 1832 as Minton-Shropshire Porcelain Company Limited; used "Minton Porcelain Company", "Shropshire Porcelain Company" and "M-S P" marks on various manufactures during 1835-1839; renamed Minton-Shropshire Unlimited in 1840). |
| 670 | ≠a Its Pseudo-porcelains, 1895. ≠b (Minton-Shropshire Porcelain Company Limited). |

**3.5.4.**

| 008 | y y m m d d n a . a c n n d a a b n . . . . . . . . . . . a . a a a . . . . . d |
| 040 | ≠a _____ ≠c _____ |
| 110 2 | ≠a National Library of Medicine (U.S.) |
| 410 1 | ≠a United States. ≠b National Library of Medicine. |
| 410 2 | ≠a National Institutes of Health (U.S.). ≠b National Library of Medicine. |
| 410 2 | ≠a NLM |

| 410 | 2 | ≠a N.L.M. |
| 670 | | ≠a U.S. Congress. Senate Committee on the Judiciary. *A National Library of Medicine: hearings, 1956.* ≠b title(National Library of Medicine) |
| 670 | | ≠a Centenary of Index Medicus, 1879-1979, 1980. ≠ b t.p. (U.S. Department of Health and Human Services, Public Health Service, National Institutes of Health, National Library of Medicine) |
| 670 | | ≠a Index of NLM serial titles, [1972]- . ≠b title (NLM) |

**3.5.5.**

| 008 | | y y m m d d n a . a c n n d a a b n . . . . . . . . . . . a . a a a . . . . . d |
| 040 | | ≠a _____ ≠c _____ |
| 110 | 2 | ≠a Public Affairs Research Council of Louisiana, inc. |
| 410 | 2 | ≠a PAR |
| 410 | 2 | ≠a P.A.R. |
| 670 | | ≠a A PAR report, 1951. ≠b t.p. (Public Affairs Research Council of Louisiana, inc.); title (PAR). |
| 678 | | ≠a Organized in 1950. |

**3.5.6.**

| 008 | | y y m m d d n a . a c n n d a a b n . . . . . . . . . . . a . a a a . . . . . d |
| 040 | | ≠a _____ ≠c _____ |
| 110 | 2 | ≠a Saint Boudreaux County Public Library. |
| 410 | 2 | ≠a St. Boudreaux County Public Library. |
| 670 | | ≠a Majors, John B. The end of the line, c1975. ≠b t.p. (Saint Boudreaux County Public Library) |

**3.5.7.**

| 008 | | y y m m d d n a . a c n n d a a b n . . . . . . . . . . a . a a a . . . . . d |
| 040 | | ≠a _____ ≠c _____ |
| 110 | 2 | ≠a Our Lady of the Mountains Undergraduate Library. |
| 410 | 2 | ≠a OLM Library. |
| 410 | 2 | ≠a Our Lady Undergraduate Library |
| 410 | 2 | ≠a University of Guadalupe Libraries. Our Lady of the Mountains Undergraduate Library. |
| 670 | | ≠a Marsh, Guinevere. University of Guadalupe Libraries, 1993. ≠b p. ii (Our Lady of the Mountains Undergraduate Library, OLM Library). |
| 670 | | ≠a Sangria, Maria. Holdings in the OLM Library, 1988 ≠b p. iv (OLM Library; Our Lady Undergraduate Library; Our Lady of the Mountains Undergraduate Library) |

### 3.5.8.

| 008 | y y m m d d n a . a c n n d a a b n . . . . . . . . . . a . a a a . . . . . d |
|-----|---|
| 040 | ≠a _____ ≠c _____ |
| 110 2 | ≠aUS3 (Music group) |
| 410 2 | ≠a US 3 (Music group) |
| 410 2 | ≠a Us Three (Music group) |
| 670 | ≠a Cedar trees of heaven [sr], 1984. ≠b CD label (US3) |
| 670 | ≠a Smith, Jim. "US 3 have made it big in the U.S.", Newsweekly, Aug. 15, 1997 (US 3; US3; Us Three) |

## Geographic Names

### 3.5.9.

| 008 | y y m m d d . a . a c a n d b a b n . . . . . . . . . . . n . a n a . . . . . d |
|-----|---|
| 040 | ≠a _____ ≠c _____ |
| 151 | ≠a Cartagena, Bay of (Colombia) |
| 451 | ≠a Bay of Cartagena (Colombia) |
| 451 | ≠a Bahia de Cartagena (Columbia) |
| 550 | ≠a Bays ≠z Columbia. |
| 670 | ≠a Willow, Diego. A multisensory picture of Cartagena Bay,Colombia, 1982. |
| 670 | ≠a LCSH, 20th ed. (1997), v.2, p. 860 (Cartagena, Bay of (Colombia), UF Bahia de Cartagena (Colombia), Bay of Cartagena (Colombia)); p. 508 (Bays (May Subd Geog)). |

### 3.5.9.

| 008 | y y m m d d . a . a c a n d b a b n . . . . . . . . . . n . a n a . . . . . d |
|-----|---|
| 040 | ≠a _____ ≠c _____ |
| 150 | ≠a Bays ≠z Columbia. |
| 551 | ≠a Cartagena, Bay of (Colombia) |
| 670 | ≠a Willow, Diego. A multisensory picture of Cartagena Bay, Colombia, 1982. |
| 670 | ≠a LCSH, 20th ed. (1997), v.1, p. 508 (Bays (May Subd Geog)), p. 860 (Cartagena, Bay of (Colombia)). |

### 3.5.10.

| 008 | y y m m d d . a . a c a n d b a b n . . . . . . . . . . n . a n a . . . . . d |
|-----|---|
| 040 | ≠a _____ ≠c _____ |
| | ≠a Khangai Mountains (Mongolia) |
| | ≠a Hangay Mountains (Mongolia) |
| | ≠a Hangayn Nuruu (Mongolia) |
| | ≠a Mountains ≠ z Mongolia |
| | ≠a Jeffries, P. Cycling the Khangai on your BMW, c2002 |

**3.5.11.**

| | |
|---|---|
| 008 | y y m m d d . a . a c a n d b a b n . . . . . . . . . . . n . a n a . . . . . d |
| 040 | ≠a _____  ≠c _____ |
| 151 | ≠a Karana (Extinct city) |
| 451 | ≠a Karana (Ancient city) |
| 451 | ≠a Tell el-Rimah (Iraq) |
| 550 | ≠a Extinct cities  ≠z Iraq. |
| 670 | ≠a Killeen, Sheila. El Souk and Karana, c1976. |
| 670 | ≠a LCSH, 20th ed. (1997), v.3, p. 2918 (Karana (Extinct City)) ; UF Karana (Ancient city), Tell el-Rimah; BT Extinct cities—Iraq. |

**3.5.11.**

| | |
|---|---|
| 008 | y y m m d d . a . a c a n d b a b n . . . . . . . . . . . n . a n a . . . . . d |
| 040 | ≠a _____  ≠c _____ |
| 150 | ≠a Extinct cities  ≠z Iraq. |
| 551 | ≠a Karana (Extinct city) |
| 670 | ≠a Killeen, Sheila. El Souk and Karana, c1976. |
| 670 | ≠a LCSH, 20th ed. (1997), v. 2, p. 1882 (Extinct cities—Iraq) : v.3, p. 2918 (Karana (Extinct City)). |

**3.5.12.**

| | |
|---|---|
| 008 | y y m m d d . a . a c a n d b a b n . . . . . . . . . . . n . a n a . . . . . d |
| 040 | ≠a _____  ≠c _____ |
| 151 | ≠a Lake District (England) |
| 451 | ≠a Lakeland (England) |
| 450 | ≠a Lakes ≠ z England. |
| 670 | ≠a Marsh, Inde. Touring the Lake District, 1994. |
| 670 | ≠a LCSH, 20th ed. (1997), v. 3, p. 3047 (Lake District (England); UF Lakeland (England), Lakes (England)) |

**3.5.13.**

| | |
|---|---|
| 008 | y y m m d d . a . a c a n d b a b n . . . . . . . . . . . n . a n a . . . . . d |
| 040 | ≠a _____  ≠c _____ |
| 151 | ≠a Mexico, Gulf of. |
| 451 | ≠a Gulf of Mexico. |
| 550 | ≠a Bays  ≠z Mexico. |
| 550 | ≠a Bays  ≠z United States. |
| 670 | ≠a Lockout, Clyde. The Gulf of Mexico, 1973. |

670        ≠a LCSH, 20th ed. (1997), v. 3, p. 3499 (Mexico, Gulf of; UF Gulf of
           Mexico; BT Bays—Mexico, Bays—United States) ; v. 1, p. 508 Bays
           (May Subd Geog)).

**3.5.13.**

008        y y m m d d . a . a c a n d b a b n . . . . . . . . . . . n . a n a . . . . . d
040        ≠a _____  ≠c _____
550        ≠a Bays  ≠z Mexico.
551        ≠a Mexico, Gulf of.
670        ≠a Lockout, Clyde. The Gulf of Mexico, 1973.
670        ≠a LCSH, 20th ed. (1997), v. 1, p. 508 (Bays (May Subd Geog)); v. 3, p. 3499
           (Mexico, Gulf of).

**3.5.13.**

008        y y m m d d . a . a c a n d b a b n . . . . . . . . . . . n . a n a . . . . . d
040        ≠a _____  ≠c _____
550        ≠a Bays  ≠z United States.
551        ≠a Mexico, Gulf of.
670        ≠a Lockout, Clyde. The Gulf of Mexico, 1973.
670        ≠a LCSH, 20th ed. (1997), v. 1, p. 508 (Bays (May Subd Geog)); v. 3, p. 3499
           (Mexico, Gulf of).

**3.5.14.**

008        y y m m d d . a . a c a n d b a b n . . . . . . . . . . . n . a n a . . . . . d
040        ≠a _____  ≠c _____
151        ≠a Mississippi River Valley.
451        ≠a Mississippi Valley.
670        ≠a Halley, B.T. Big Father of Waters, 1989 (Mississippi River, Mississippi
           Valley).
670        ≠a LCSH, 20th ed. (1997), v. 3, p. 3563 (Mississippi River Valley; UF
           Mississippi Valley).

**3.5.15.**

008        y y m m d d . a . a c a n d b a b n . . . . . . . . . . n . a n a . . . . . d
040        ≠a _____  ≠c _____
151        ≠a Pontchartrain, Lake (La.)
451        ≠a Lake Pontchartrain (La.)
550        ≠a Lakes  ≠z Louisiana.
670        ≠a Jones, Billy Bob. Lake Pontchartrain, c1954.
670        ≠a LCSH, 20th ed. (1997), v. 3, p. 4356 (Pontchartrain, Lake (La.); UF Lake
           Pontchartrain (La.); BT Lakes —Louisiana).

**3.5.15.**

| | |
|---|---|
| 008 | y y m m d d . a . a c a n d b a b n . . . . . . . . . . . n . a n a . . . . . d |
| 040 | ≠a _____ ≠c _____ |
| 150 | ≠a Lakes ≠z Louisiana. |
| 551 | ≠a Pontchartrain, Lake (La.) |
| 670 | ≠a Jones, Billy Bob. Lake Pontchartrain, c1954 |
| 670 | ≠a LCSH, 20th ed. (1997), v. 3, p. 3051 (Lakes (May Subd Geog)); p. 4356 (Pontchartrain, Lake (La.). |

**3.5.16.**

| | |
|---|---|
| 008 | y y m m d d . a . a c a n d b a b n . . . . . . . . . . . n . a n a . . . . . d |
| 040 | ≠a _____ ≠c _____ |
| 151 | ≠a Salmon River, Middle Fork (Idaho) |
| 451 | ≠a Middle Fork, Salmon River (Idaho) |
| 550 | ≠a Rivers ≠z Idaho. |
| 670 | ≠a Zines, Winfred. Middle Fork of the Salmon, c1980. |
| 670 | ≠a LCSH, 20th ed. (1997) v. 4, p. 4853 (Salmon River, Middle Fork (Idaho); UF Middle Fork, Salmon River (Idaho); BT Rivers—Idaho)) |

**3.5.16.**

| | |
|---|---|
| 008 | y y m m d d . a . a c a n d b a b n . . . . . . . . . . . n . a n a . . . . . d |
| 040 | ≠a _____ ≠c _____ |
| 150 | ≠a Rivers ≠z Idaho. |
| 551 | ≠a Salmon River, Middle Fork (Idaho) |
| 670 | ≠a Zines, Winfred. Middle Fork of the Salmon, c1980. |
| 670 | ≠a LCSH, 20th ed. (1997) v. 4, p. 4734 (Rivers (May Subd Geog)); p. 4853 (Salmon River, Middle Fork (Idaho)). |

## Personal Names

**3.5.17.**

| | | |
|---|---|---|
| 008 | | y y m m d d n a . a c n n d a a b n . . . . . . . . . . . a . a a a . . . . . d |
| 040 | | ≠a _____ ≠c _____ |
| 100 | 1 | ≠a W, Mickey. |
| 400 | 1 | ≠a Jones, Michael. |
| 400 | 1 | ≠a Mullins, Al. |
| 670 | | ≠a Encyclopedic dictionary of African-Americans, c1975 (Mickey W., born 1/1/42, d. 2/2/70; b. as Michael Jones; also known as Big Al Mullins). |

**3.5.18.**

| 008 | y y m m d d n a . a c n n d a a b n . . . . . . . . . . a . a a a . . . . . d |
|---|---|
| 040 | ≠a _____  ≠c _____ |
| 100 1 | ≠a Davis, Jimmie, ≠d 1902- |
| 400 1 | ≠a Davis, James Houston, ≠d 1902- |
| 510 1 | ≠a Louisiana. ≠b Governor (1944-1948 : Davis) |
| 510 1 | ≠a Louisiana. ≠b Governor (1960-1964 : Davis) |
| 670 | ≠a His Louisiana, here I come!, 1963 (Jimmie Davis) |
| 670 | ≠a His You are my sunshine, 1985 (James Houston Davis; b. 9/11/1902; governor of Louisiana 1944-48, 1960-64). |
| 678 | ≠a Preferred to be known as Jimmie. |

**3.5.18.**

| 008 | y y m m d d n a . a c n n d a a b n . . . . . . . . . . a . a a a . . . . . d |
|---|---|
| 040 | ≠a _____  ≠c _____ |
| 110 1 | ≠a Louisiana. ≠b Governor (1944-1948 : Davis) |
| 510 1 | ≠a Louisiana. ≠b Governor (1960-1964 : Davis) |
| 500 1 | ≠a Davis, Jimmie, ≠d 1902- |
| 670 | ≠a His Louisiana, here I come!, 1963 (Jimmie Davis) |
| 670 | ≠a His You are my sunshine, 1985 (James Houston Davis; b. 9/11/1902; governor of Louisiana 1944-48, 1960-64). |
| 678 | ≠a Preferred to be known as Jimmie. |

**3.5.18.**

| 008 | y y m m d d n a . a c n n d a a b n . . . . . . . . . . a . a a a . . . . . d |
|---|---|
| 040 | ≠a _____  ≠c _____ |
| 110 1 | ≠a Louisiana. ≠ b Governor (1960-1964 : Davis) |
| 510 1 | ≠a Louisiana. ≠b Governor (1944-1948 : Davis) |
| 500 1 | ≠a Davis, Jimmie, ≠d 1902- |
| 670 | ≠a His Louisiana, here I come!, 1963 (Jimmie Davis. |
| 670 | ≠a His You are my sunshine, 1985 Louisiana, 1972 (James Houston Davis; b. 9/11/1902; governor of Louisiana 1944-48, 1960-64). |
| 678 | ≠a Preferred to be known as Jimmie. |

**3.5.19.**

| 008 | y y m m d d n a . a c n n d a a b n . . . . . . . . . . a . a a a . . . . . d |
|---|---|
| 040 | ≠a _____  ≠c _____ |
| 100 1 | ≠a Huey, John, ≠d 1874-1969. |
| 400 1 | ≠a Smith, Charles John Huey, ≠d 1874-1969. |
| 500 1 | ≠a Smith, Charles, ≠d 1874-1969. |

| 670 | ≠a His The extraneous murders, c1923. ≠b t.p. (John Huey). |
| 670 | ≠a Contemptuous authors, v. 1195 (b. 3/29/1874, d. 8/28/1969; b. as Charles John Huey Smith; also wrote as Charles Smith) |

**3.5.19.**

| 008 | y y m m d d n a . a c n n d a a b n . . . . . . . . . . . a . a a a . . . . . d |
| 040 | ≠a _____ ≠c _____ |
| 100 1 | ≠a Smith, Charles, ≠d 1874-1969. |
| 400 1 | ≠a Smith, Charles John Huey, ≠d 1874-1969. |
| 500 1 | ≠a Huey, John, ≠d 1874-1969. |
| 670 | ≠a His The extraneous murders, c1923. ≠ b t.p. (Charles Smith) |
| 670 | ≠a Contemptuous authors, v. 1195 (b. 3/29/1874, d. 8/28/1969; b. as Charles John Huey Smith; also wrote as John Huey) |

**3.5.20.**

| 008 | y y m m d d n a . a c n n d a a b n . . . . . . . . . . . a . a a a . . . . . d |
| 040 | ≠a _____ ≠c _____ |
| 100 1 | ≠a Gogh, Vincent van, ≠d 1853-1890. |
| 400 1 | ≠a Van Gogh, Vincent, ≠d 1853-1890. |
| 400 1 | ≠a Gogh, Vincent-Willem van, ≠d 1853-1890. |
| 670 | ≠a His Tableaux, aquarelles, dessin..., 1904. |
| 670 | ≠a Vincent van Gogh (1853-1890), 1958: (Vincent-Willem van Gogh, b. 3/30/1853; d. 7/29/1890). |

**3.5.21.**

| 008 | y y m m d d n a . a c n n d a a b n . . . . . . . . . . . a . a a a . . . . . d |
| 040 | ≠a _____ ≠c _____ |
| 100 1 | ≠a Lambert-Pitcherly, Carolyn. |
| 400 1 | ≠a Pitcherly, Carolyn Lambert. |
| 670 | ≠a Her First you must make the roux, c1991 (Carolyn Lambert Pitcherly) |
| 670 | ≠a Great chefs of the South, 1999 (Carolyn Lambert Pitcherly) |

**3.5.22.**

| 008 | y y m m d d n a . a c n n d a a b n . . . . . . . . . . . a . a a a . . . . . d |
| 040 | ≠a _____ ≠c _____ |
| 100 1 | ≠a Bentley, Susan L. |
| 400 1 | ≠a Bentley, Sue. |
| 670 | ≠a Her Avoyelles Parish, the happy parish, c1979 (Susan L. Bentley) |
| 670 | ≠a Lewis, M.L. III Coushatta and the Indians, c1994 (Sue Bentley). |

**3.5.23.**

| | | |
|---|---|---|
| 008 | | y y m m d d n a . a c n n d a a b n . . . . . . . . . . a . a a a . . . . . d |
| 040 | | ≠a _____ ≠c _____ |
| 100 | 1 | ≠a Bartholomew, Don, ≠d 1963- |
| 400 | 1 | ≠a Bartholomew, Donald Henry, ≠ d 1963- |
| 670 | | ≠a Don Bartholomew's Mongolia, c1996. |
| 670 | | ≠a Phone call to author, 5/16/96: full name is Donald Henry Bartholomew; born in Ulaanbaatar, Mongolia, on 1/25/63; usage: Don Bartholomew). |

**3.5.24.**

| | | |
|---|---|---|
| 008 | | y y m m d d n a . a c n n d a a b n . . . . . . . . . . a . a a a . . . . . d |
| 040 | | ≠a _____ ≠c _____ |
| 100 | 1 | ≠a Ward, Humphry, ≠c Mrs., ≠d 1851-1920. |
| 400 | 1 | ≠a Ward, Mary Augusta Arnold, ≠d 1851-1920. |
| 400 | 1 | ≠a Arnold, Mary Augusta, ≠d 1851-1920. |
| 670 | | ≠a Her Helbeck of Bannisdale, 1883 (Mrs. Humphry Ward, b. Mary Augusta Arnold; in T'bilisi, Georgia, 1851) |
| 670 | | ≠a Oxford companion to English literature, 1985 (Mary Augusta Ward; d. 1920) |
| 678 | | ≠a Native of  T'bilisi,Georgia. |

## Topical Subject Headings

**3.5.25.**

| | |
|---|---|
| 008 | y y m m d d n a . a c a n d b a b n . . . . . . . . . . n . a n a . . . . . d |
| 040 | ≠a _____ ≠c _____ |
| 150 | ≠a Heraldry. |
| 450 | ≠a Coats of arms. |
| 450 | ≠a Blazonry. |
| 450 | ≠a Arms, Coats of. |
| 670 | ≠a Brault, G. J. Early blazon, c1972. |
| 670 | ≠a LCSH, 20th ed. (1997), v. 2, p. 2443 (Heraldry; UF Arms, Coats of, Blazonry, Coats of arms). |

**3.5.26.**

| | |
|---|---|
| 008 | y y m m d d n a . a c a n d b a b n . . . . . . . . . . n . a n a . . . . . d |
| 040 | ≠a _____ ≠c _____ |
| 150 | ≠a Hounds. |
| 450 | ≠a Catahoula hounds. |
| 450 | ≠a Catahoula leopard dog. |
| 450 | ≠a Catahoula hog dog. |

| 670 | ≠a Jenkins, Huey. Encyclopedia of the Catahoula hound, c1992. |
|---|---|
| 670 | ≠a Brown, W.C. The Catahoula hog dog, 1962. |
| 670 | ≠a LCSH, 20th ed. (1997), v. 2, p. 2537 (Hounds). |

**3.5.27.**

| 008 | y y m m d d n a . a c a n d b a b n . . . . . . . . . . n . a n a . . . . . d |
|---|---|
| 040 | ≠a _____  ≠c _____ |
| 150 | ≠a Mental fatigue. |
| 450 | ≠a Exhaustion, Mental. |
| 450 | ≠a Fatigue, Mental. |
| 450 | ≠a Mental overwork. |
| 670 | ≠a Green, W.J. Fatigue free, c1992. |
| 670 | ≠a Ferguson, Bobby. How to catalog with joy, c1999. |

**3.5.28.**

| 008 | y y m m d d n a . a c a n d b a b n . . . . . . . . . . n . a n a . . . . . d |
|---|---|
| 040 | ≠a _____  ≠c _____ |
| 150 | ≠a Rose culture. |
| 450 | ≠a Rose growing. |
| 670 | ≠a Baker, M.L. Roses and their culture, c1991. |
| 670 | ≠a LCSH, 20th ed. (1997), v. 4, p. 4788 (Rose culture; UF Rose growing) |

**3.5.29.**

| 008 | y y m m d d n a . a c a n d b a b n . . . . . . . . . . n . a n a . . . . . d |
|---|---|
| 040 | ≠a _____  ≠c _____ |
| 150 | ≠a Rhodesian ridgeback. |
| 450 | ≠a Ridgeback, Rhodesian. |
| 450 | ≠a African lion hound. |
| 450 | ≠a Lion hound, African. |
| 550 | ≠a Hounds. |
| 670 | ≠a Linzy, J. Rhodesian ridgeback champions, 1955-1980, c1981. |
| 670 | ≠a LCSH, 20th ed. (1997), v. 4, p. 4707 (Rhodesian ridgeback; UF African lion hound; Lion hound, African; Ridgeback, Rhodesian; BT Hounds) |

**3.5.29.**

| 008 | y y m m d d n a . a c a n d b a b n . . . . . . . . . . n . a n a . . . . . d |
|---|---|
| 040 | ≠a _____  ≠c _____ |
| 150 | ≠a Hounds. |
| 550 | ≠a Rhoesian ridgeback. |
| 450 | ≠a Lion hound, African. |

| | |
|---|---|
| 670 | ≠a Jeffries, Prince. Hounds of the world, c1975. |
| 670 | ≠a LCSH, 20th ed. (1997), v. 2, p. 2537 (Hounds; BT Dog breeds) |

**3.5.30.**

| | |
|---|---|
| 008 | y y m m d d n a . a c a n d b a b n . . . . . . . . . . n . a n a . . . . . d |
| 040 | ≠a _____  ≠c _____ |
| 150 | ≠a Theology. |
| 450 | ≠a Christian theology. |
| 450 | ≠a Theology, Christian. |
| 550 | ≠a Theology, Doctrinal. |
| 550 | ≠a Theology, Practical. |
| 670 | ≠a Montefiore, H. Credible Christianity, c1994. |
| 670 | ≠a LCSH, 20th ed. (1997), v. 4, p 5548 (Theology; UF Christian theology; Theology, Christian; NT Theology, Doctrinal; Theology, Practical). |

**3.5.30.**

| | |
|---|---|
| 008 | y y m m d d n a . a c a n d b a b n . . . . . . . . . . n . a n a . . . . . d |
| 040 | ≠a _____  ≠c _____ |
| 150 | ≠a Theology, Doctrinal. |
| 550 | ≠a Theology. |
| 550 | ≠a Theology, Practical. |
| 670 | ≠a Montefiore, H. Credible Christianity, c1994 |
| 670 | ≠a LCSH, 20th ed. (1997), v. 4, p 5548 (Theology; UF Christian theology; Theology, Christian; NT Theology, Doctrinal; Theology, Practical). |

**3.5.30.**

| | |
|---|---|
| 008 | y y m m d d n a . a c a n d b a b n . . . . . . . . . . n . a n a . . . . . d |
| 040 | ≠a _____  ≠c _____ |
| 150 | ≠a Theology, Practical. |
| 550 | ≠a Theology, Doctrinal. |
| 550 | ≠a Theology. |
| 670 | ≠a Montefiore, H. Credible Christianity, c1994. |
| 670 | ≠a LCSH, 20th ed. (1997), v. 4, p 5548 (Theology; UF Christian theology; Theology, Christian; NT Theology, Doctrinal; Theology, Practical). |

**3.5.31.**

| | |
|---|---|
| 008 | y y m m d d n a . a c a n d b a b n . . . . . . . . . . n . a n a . . . . . d |
| 040 | ≠a _____  ≠c _____ |
| 150 | ≠a Wreaths. |
| 450 | ≠a Garlands. |

| | |
|---|---|
| 550 | ≠a Handicraft. |
| 670 | ≠a Pflumm, C.C. Hearthstrings, c1993. |
| 670 | ≠a LCSH, 20th ed. (1997), v. 4, p. 6096 (Wreaths; UF Garlands; BT Handicraft). |

**3.5.31.**

| | |
|---|---|
| 008 | y y m m d d n a . a c a n d b a b n . . . . . . . . . . . n . a n a . . . . . d |
| 040 | ≠a _____  ≠c _____ |
| 150 | ≠a Handicraft. |
| 550 | ≠a Wreaths. |
| 670 | ≠a Pflumm, C.C. Hearthstrings, c1993. |
| 670 | ≠a LCSH, 20th ed. (1997), v. 2, p. 2377 (Handicraft); v. 4, p. 6096 (Wreaths). |

**3.5.32.**

| | |
|---|---|
| 008 | y y m m d d n a . a c a n d b a b n . . . . . . . . . . . n . a n a . . . . . d |
| 040 | ≠a _____  ≠c _____ |
| 150 | ≠a Acrylic painting. |
| 450 | ≠a Polymer painting. |
| 450 | ≠a Synthetic painting. |
| 670 | ≠a Taubes, F. Acrylic painting for the beginner, c1971. |
| 670 | ≠a LCSH, 20th ed. (1997), v. 1, p. 34 (Acrylic painting; UF Polymer painting, Synthetic painting). |

# ABOUT THE AUTHOR

BOBBY FERGUSON is Head of Technical Services, East Baton Rouge Parish Library, Louisiana.